A Bluestocking Guide

Applying the
Clipper Ship Strategy

by

Kathryn Daniels

based on Richard J. Maybury's book
THE CLIPPER SHIP STRATEGY

published by
Bluestocking Press

web site: www.BluestockingPress.com
Phone 800-959-8586

Printed and bound in the United States of America.
Cover illustration by Bob O'Hara, Georgetown, CA
Cover design by Brian C. Williams, El Dorado, CA
Edited by Jane A. Williams

ISBN-10: 0-942617-50-9
ISBN-13: 978-0-942617-50-4

Published by

Bluestocking Press • Post Office Box 1014
Placerville, CA 95667-1014 • Phone: 800-959-8586
web site: www.BluestockingPress.com

Quantity Discounts Available

Books published by Bluestocking Press are available at special quantity discounts for bulk purchases to individuals, businesses, schools, libraries, and associations, to be distributed as gifts, premiums, or as fund raisers.

For terms and discount schedule contact:

Special Sales Department
Bluestocking Press
Phone: 800-959-8586
email: CustomerService@BluestockingPress.com
web site: www.BluestockingPress.com

Specify how books are to be distributed: for classrooms, or as gifts, premiums, fund raisers—or to be resold.

Contents

Chapter Title	Questions	Answers

Part 1 — Sales Strategy

Chapter Title	**Questions**	**Answers**

Part 2 — Production Strategy

Bluestocking Guides are designed to reinforce and enhance a student's understanding of the subject presented in the primer. The subject for this study guide is business cycle management. The primer is THE CLIPPER SHIP STRATEGY by Richard J. Maybury.

Given the wide range of age and ability levels of individuals who read THE CLIPPER SHIP STRATEGY, it is suggested that students complete the exercises in this study guide that are most age-appropriate or ability-appropriate for them.

Assignment of Exercises

While all given questions and assignments are designed to enhance the student's understanding and retention of the subject matter presented in the primer, it is by no means mandatory that each student complete every exercise in this study guide. This study guide is designed for flexibility based on a student's age, as well as a student's interest in the material presented.

It is strongly suggested that each student complete the Comprehension Exercises, but instructors can preview and then select the Application Exercises, Films to View, and Suggested Books to Read that they wish the student to complete, based on: course time available, student's interest, and/or student's age (some films/books might not be age appropriate — the student might be too young, too old, or the content too advanced for a younger student). Also, depending on the age and interest level of a student, one student might spend weeks on a research assignment, whereas another student might spend a few hours or days.

Suggested Time Frame For Study

This study guide is organized to allow the instructor flexibility in designing the ideal course of study. Therefore, there is no "right" or "wrong" time frame for covering the material; the instructor should tailor the study of the primer and study guide to the student's unique school schedule, learning style, and age. For example, younger students may only complete comprehension exercises, whereas older students may complete additional application exercises, suggested readings, and films.

An easy-to-apply rule of thumb for determining length of study is to divide the number of chapters in a primer by the number of weeks the instructor plans to study the subject/book.

Ideally, the student should read a chapter from the primer and then immediately answer the corresponding questions in the study guide. Chapter length varies, so sometimes a student may be able to read more than one chapter and complete the corresponding questions/exercises in a day. Some instructors may choose to complete the primer in a few short weeks in which case multiple chapters per day will need to be covered. Others may plan to study the primer over an entire semester, so only a few chapters per week will be assigned. The key is to move quickly enough that the student is engaged with learning and also able to absorb all concepts fully. The student's performance on end-of-chapter Questions and Assignments should be a good indication of this.

The time frame for completing application exercises (Discussion/Essay/Assignment/Research) is also subject to the instructor's discretion. Most discussions can take place immediately after reading the chapter. However, students may need a day or two to complete an essay, and some assignments will take outside research requiring additional time. It is best for the instructor to preview the application exercises (Discussion/Essay/Assignment/Research) and assign the student a "due date" based upon the student's cognitive abilities and available course schedule.

Comprehension Exercises

Comprehension Exercises test the degree to which the student understands and retains the information presented in each chapter. In this study guide Comprehension Exercises include: 1) Define, 2) True/False, and 3) Short Answer/Fill-In. Students are encouraged to answer all exercises in complete sentences. The information needed to complete these exercises can usually be found in the given chapter of the primer. Answers will be found in the answer section of this Study Guide.

Define

The student should define the given term based on Richard Maybury's definition provided in the given chapter or glossary (*not* a standard dictionary definition). This is essential. As Richard Maybury says, "Fuzzy language causes fuzzy thinking." For any discussion or explanation to be clearly understood, one must first understand the intended definition of words as used by the author. Confusion and disagreement can occur because the student does not understand the author's intended definition of a word. To reinforce this point, have a student look up the word "law" in an unabridged Webster's dictionary. The student should find a number of definitions following the word "law." Again, unless one agrees on the definition intended for the discussion or study at hand, misunderstanding or "fuzzy thinking" can result.

True/False

For True/False exercises, if the student believes the statement is correct, the student should simply write "True" as the answer. If the student believes the statement is *not* true, the student should write "False." If the student answers the question "False," the student should be sure to state why the statement is *not* true or rewrite the false statement to make it true. In the answer section of this study guide, statements that are "False" are so noted and have been rewritten to make them true.

Short Answer/Fill In

The student should answer Short Answer/Fill In questions based upon knowledge gained from studying the given chapter. Unless the student is asked to use his/her own opinion or knowledge, the answer should be based upon Richard Maybury's statements. Generally, Short Answer/Fill In Questions are selected verbatim from the given chapter.

Application Exercises

With few exceptions, Application Exercises ask the student to apply the knowledge and ideas he/she has gained from a given chapter to "real world" situations. In many cases, these assignments are designed to help the student personalize the information just learned so that the student can better retain and apply the knowledge. In this study guide application exercises include: 1) Discussion, 2) Essay, 3) Assignment, and 4) For Further Research. In the majority of instances, answers to Application Exercises will vary based upon the student's own experiences. Application Exercises are designed to encourage informal discussions among students and instructors, and/or to stimulate students to critically evaluate the scenario. However, the instructor may ask the student to write answers (in essay format, outline, etc.) if a more formal/structure approach is desired.

For Further Reading or To View

The books and films mentioned in For Further Reading and To View are designed to expand students' understanding of concepts presented in the related chapter. No written or verbal reports on the books/movies are usually required, however, students and instructors are encouraged to discuss the ideas presented. Thus, Suggestions for Further Reading/Viewing usually have no set answers and, therefore, may not appear in the "Answer" section. (The instructor may choose to assign a book/movie report of his/her own construction if he/she desires.)

How to Grade Assignments

Define, True/False, Short Answer/Fill-In

To determine the percentage of correct answers, divide the total number of correct answers by the total number of questions. If, for example, a chapter section has two Define questions, one True/False question, and seven Short Answer/Fill-In questions, and the student has answered correctly eight of these questions, the student will have answered 80% of the questions correctly.

$$8 \div 10 = .80 \ (\text{or} \ 80\%)$$

Number of Correct Answers ÷ Number of Total Questions
= Percentage of Questions Answered Correctly

In "Grade" equivalents, percentage scores generally range as follows:

90 - 100%	= A
80 - 89.9%	= B
70 - 79.9%	= C
60 - 69.9%	= D
less than 60%	= F

In general, a student earning an "A" has demonstrated excellent understanding of the subject matter; a student earning a "B" has demonstrated good understanding of the subject matter; a student earning a "C" has demonstrated sufficient understanding of the subject matter; and a student earning a "D" or "F" would benefit from reviewing the subject matter to strengthen his/her understanding of the topic at hand.

In determining whether a student has provided a "right" or "wrong" answer to a question, the instructor should compare the student's answers with the answers provided in this guide. True/False, Fill-In, and Define questions/answers are straightforward. Short Answer questions/answers are also generally straightforward; on some longer answers the student's wording may vary slightly from the answer provided in this study guide, but the student should receive full credit if the *content* of his/her answer is correct. When in doubt, it is recommended that the instructor refer back to the chapter in the primary text to reference what the author said about the issue at hand.

"Answers Will Vary"

In the answer section of this study guide you will sometimes come across an answer that reads "answers will vary" for a given question. This generally means that the student is required to answer the question using his/her own knowledge, experience, or intuition. In these instances, the instructor should refer back to the chapter in the primary text to reference what the author said about the issue at hand compared to the student's answer; a "correct" answer should be thoughtful, complete, and on-topic.

Discussion/Essay/Assignment

These assignments are provided so that students can apply the concepts they learned in the given chapter to their own experiences, current events, or historical events — to make the concepts more meaningful. In most cases, it is extremely difficult to "grade" the completed assignments as "right" or "wrong." Instead, the instructor should provide guidance for these assignments. The completeness, thoughtfulness, enthusiasm, and meaning the student brings to the assignment will serve as an indication of the student's mastery of the assignment. If the instructor then wishes to assign a grade, he/she may elect to do so. Or, these assignments may be non-graded "extra credit," serving to boost the student's overall grade for the course.

Uncle Eric's Model of How the World Works

Short Answer/Fill-In/True or False

1. What is a model as defined by Uncle Eric?

2. According to Uncle Eric, why are models important?

3. Why is it important to sort incoming data?

4. Are models rigid? Should they ever change?

5. What are the two models Uncle Eric believes are most reliable, as well as crucially important for everyone to learn? Why does he believe this?

6. _____ is the political philosophy that is no philosophy at all. It embraces the concept that those in power can do whatever appears necessary to achieve their goals.

Discussion/Essay/Assignment

7. Other than Uncle Eric's model, can you provide other examples of models?

8. What purpose does the book THE CLIPPER SHIP STRATEGY have relative to Uncle Eric's Model?

9. Listen to, or read, politicians' political speeches, news conferences, news releases, etc., and note if, or how often, the politicians use the phrase "we will do whatever is necessary" to execute a proposal, fix a problem, etc. Do you think it is ever okay to "do whatever is necessary" to resolve a problem? Explain your answer.

10. Look up several of the following words in a dictionary and read their definitions: fascism, liberty, economics, history, republic, and democracy. Does each word have more than one definition? Why?

11. If a word has more than one definition, why is it important that an author define his/her meaning of a word about which he/she is writing?

12. Richard Feynman, a Nobel prize winning physicist, once said it didn't matter what something was called, so long as one understood the characteristics that go into making up what that thing is. It doesn't matter if we call the bird identified as a Blue Jay, a "Blue Jay," so long as we understand that the living creature called by that name has the following characteristics: The bird's food consists primarily of nuts and small seeds as well as insects. They lay from three to six eggs that are blue, green, or yellow with spots of brown or gray. They live for about four years. Another example might be: You might have different names during your lifetime, but you are still the same person. When you are born your parents might name you William. As a child, you might be Billy, or you might

be given a nickname (i.e. Laura Ingalls Wilder from the LITTLE HOUSE™ books was called Half-pint by her Pa). As a teenager you might be Bill or Will, then, as an adult, you might use the more formal William. In all these cases, with all these names, you are still you. If you are female, you might have a maiden name and a married name. Do you agree or disagree with Richard Feynman? Does it matter what something is called, so long as one understands the characteristics of the thing? Explain and provide support for your position.

For Further Reading

13.   Read CAPITALISM FOR KIDS by Karl Hess for additional information on different political philosophies, particularly the chapter called "Capitalism and Other Isms." Published by Bluestocking Press, web site: www.BluestockingPress.com; Phone: 800-959-8586.

Author's Disclosure

Short Answer/Fill-In/True or False

1.   What is Juris Naturalism?

Discussion/Essay/Assignment

2.   In the "Author's Disclosure," Richard Maybury says that few writers disclose the viewpoints or opinions they use to decide what information is important and what is not, or what data will be presented and what data omitted. Collect several history books from your home library, school library, or public library. Do the authors of the books you collected disclose their viewpoints or opinions to the reader? Do the authors disclose what criteria they used to determine what information or data to include in the book and what to omit? Explain why it is, or is not, important to have biases disclosed. What benefit, if any, does a reader or viewer have (in the case of movies, televised news, or documentaries) if he/she is able to determine the viewpoint of a writer?

3.   Uncle Eric says all history is slanted based on the facts historians choose to report. Can you provide examples of material you have read or to which you have listened where facts have been reported but perhaps not all the facts? If no books come to mind, have you had arguments or disagreements between siblings or friends in which, when asked, each person presented his/her side of the argument—presenting only those facts that best favored his/her side of the story? How can you learn to identify the slants of writers, news commentators, friends, etc.?

4.   Read the quotes in the "Author's Disclosure" section of this book that help to describe the Juris Naturalist viewpoint. Look up the definition of "unalienable" in a current dictionary. Compare a current dictionary's definition with the definition from NOAH WEBSTER'S 1828 DICTIONARY: "Unalienable; that cannot be legally or justly alienated or transferred to another ... All men have certain natural rights which are inalienable."

5.   Samuel Adams defined the natural rights of the colonists as the right to life, liberty, and property. Why do you think "property" was changed to "happiness" in the Declaration of Independence? *(Optional exercise: You can turn this into a research exercise by researching primary source documents of America's Founders to see if you can find the answer for the change from "property" to "happiness." Provide support for your position.)*

6.   Select one of the quotes from the "Author's Disclosure" section of this book and write a short essay about what the quote means to you.

For Further Reading

7.   Read HOW TO LIE WITH STATISTICS by Darrell Huff, published by W.W. Norton and distributed by Bluestocking Press, web site: www.BluestockingPress.com; Phone: 800-959-8586. A modern classic. Excellent book. Shows how statistics can distort truth. For ages 14 and up.

8.   Read EVALUATING BOOKS: WHAT WOULD THOMAS JEFFERSON THINK ABOUT THIS? an Uncle Eric book by Richard J. Maybury. This book provides key indicators and terms to help the reader learn how to identify the slants of authors, media commentators, and others. Published by Bluestocking Press, web site: www.BluestockingPress.com; Phone: 800-959-8586. For ages 12 and up.

9.   Visit www.Worldpress.org on the Internet. Many articles posted on this site list the author and his/her philosophical viewpoint, i.e., Centrist, Libertarian, Liberal, Conservative. Have someone cover up the name and philosophical identity of each author and then read the articles. Can you identify each author's philosophical viewpoint? For help with this exercise, if a student has limited knowledge of political and economic biases, the student should first read Richard J. Maybury's books: EVALUATING BOOKS: WHAT WOULD THOMAS JEFFERSON THINK ABOUT THIS? and ARE YOU LIBERAL? CONSERVATIVE? OR CONFUSED? published by Bluestocking Press.

The CARS Checklist for Research Source Evaluation

Credibility • Accuracy • Reasonableness • Support

The CARS checklist is designed to provide criteria for evaluating the quality and reliability of a source. By applying the CARS checklist you will be better able to separate high-quality from poor quality information to any research you conduct. You will be better prepared to critically evaluate data and expert opinions, which will better equip you to excel in school, career, and life. Read more about the CARS checklist for Research Source Evaluation at one or more of the Internet sites below. (If these sites are no longer available, then conduct an Internet search for "CARS checklist" and click on a university/college link to an explanatory article.)

http://www.virtualsalt.com/evalu8it.htm
www.ru.ac.za/library/infolit/cars.html
http://www.mhhe.com/socscience/english/allwrite3/seyler/ssite/seyler/se03/cars.mhtml

Thought Exercises

Before you begin to read THE CLIPPER SHIP STRATEGY, answer the following questions. Your answers should be based on your current knowledge and/or opinions. (If you have no knowledge of the issue/topic, say so.) Save your responses. You will revisit these questions at a later time. After you have answered the questions, you may begin to read THE CLIPPER SHIP STRATEGY.

1. List reasons why a business fails.

2. List reasons why a business succeeds.

3. Get two sheets of paper. On one sheet place the heading "Employee." On another sheet of paper place the heading "Self-employed." Below each header (on both sheets of paper) make two columns. Head the first column with the word "Pros" and head the second column with the word "Cons." Next, list all the positive and negative reasons you can think of for being an employee versus being self-employed.

Employee	
Pros	Cons
1.	1.
2.	2.
3.	3.
4.	4.
5.	5.

Self-Employed	
Pros	Cons
1.	1.
2.	2.
3.	3.
4.	4.
5.	5.

4. What role, if any, does government play in the success or failure of businesses? Explain your answer.

5. Identify one of the safest geographical locations to start a business or look for a job. Explain the reason for your choice.

Part 1: Sales Strategy

Chapter 1: A Strategy for Success

Define

1. Economics:

2. Business Cycle Management (BCM):

3. Recession:

4. Economy:

5. Boom-and-Bust Cycle:

6. Injection Effect:

7. Business Cycle:

8. Money Supply:

9. Velocity:

10. Money Demand:

11. Theory:

12. Application:

13. Statist:

14. Laws:

Short Answer/Fill-in/True or False

15. What was the *Flying Cloud?*

16. True or False: In bad times as well as good, someone is always earning money. (Also provide an example to support your answer.)

17. Why is it important to start incorporating the business cycle management (BCM) model into a person's daily way of looking at the world?

Discussion/Essay/Assignment

18. In this letter, Uncle Eric explains why it is important for you to begin to incorporate the BCM model into the way you look at the world around you — especially the business world. How do you currently view the business world and your own finances? Do you follow the events on Wall Street? What system do you use to manage your money now?

Chapter 2: Ethics and the Flood of Data

Define

1. Zero Sum Game:

2. Wealth:

3. Money:

4. Model:

Short Answer/Fill-in/True or False

5. The first two important points in the discussion of BCM are _____ .

6. When considering the ethics of BCM and the injection effect, what must you remember?

7. What is the difference between wealth and money?

8. Is the economy a zero sum game? Why or why not?

9. How do models help us?

Discussion/Essay/Assignment

10. In this chapter, Uncle Eric introduces the concept of *models*. Models are our most important tool in knowing what information is important and what is not. He provides an example of this—the football game story. For the rest of the day, try to determine how many times you apply the concept of models to information you receive. Perhaps you watch television, read a newspaper or magazine, or have a conversation with family or friends. Later in the day try to recollect the things you heard/read. What do you remember? What have you forgotten? How did models help with this? (For example, if your friend mentions that his/her cousin's birthday is next week, you might not remember that. But if your friend mentions that *his/her* birthday is next week you will probably remember—it is important to you because of your relationship with your friend. Your model for friendship tells you that remembering a friend's birthday is an important component to being a good friend).

Chapter 3: Hot Spots and Evidence

Define

1. "Real" Money Supply:

2. The Federal Reserve (the Fed):

3. Discount Rate:

4. Hot Spots:

5. Evidence:

6. Forecasts:

7. Shares of Stock:

8. Standards of Proof:

9. Price:

10. Bull Market:

11. Bear Market:

Short Answer/Fill-in/True or False

12. Explain how money descends on the economy.

13. Do hot spots remain constant?

14. What is the difference between evidence and forecasts as applicable to business situations (i.e., buying shares of stock)?

15. True or False: When lots of people who know nothing about something are buying it, that is a good time to sell it. Why or why not?

Discussion/Essay/Assignment

16. Construct a timeline or timetable of the major economic events from 1970 to 1990 based on Uncle Eric's discussion in this chapter.

Chapter 4: Austrian Economics

Define

1. Cold Spot:

2. Austrian Economics:

3. Keynesian Economics:

4. Monetarist Economics:

5. Cones:

6. Ecology (as it relates to the economy):

Short Answer/Fill-in/True or False

7. Why are the examples in Uncle Eric's letters drawn mostly from the period 1970 to 1990?

8. Few of today's business people have studied the concepts of free-market Austrian economics. Most have studied Keynesian or Monetarist economics. Why?

9. What is one of the strengths in Monetarist economics?

10. What is one of the weaknesses in Austrian economics, as well as other economic models?

11. What makes Austrian economics different from other schools of economics?

12. True or False: Free-market "Austrian" economics is the only type of economics that has done a thorough investigation of the injection effect?

Discussion/Essay/Assignment

13. Uncle Eric claims that most people in America today are unfamiliar with the concept of free-market "Austrian" economics and its founders Nobel Laureate F.A. Hayek and Ludwig von Mises. He urges Chris to test this claim. You can, too. Try asking your parents, friends, and any businesspersons you meet about Austrian economics. Note how many are familiar with Austrian economics. Ask those that are familiar with Austrian economics where and how they heard about it and whether they use it in their personal and business lives.

14. Many people have never learned about economics or were confused by the economics they were taught. Most are unaware that different schools of economic thought exist. Test this yourself. Ask those who are willing to help you if they are aware that different schools of economic thought exist and if so, can they name and explain any of them (Austrian, Keynesian, Monetarist).

Chapter 5: Line and Staff

Define

1. Line Functions:

2. Staff Functions:

3. Production Function:

4. Sales Function:

5. Clipper Ship Strategy:

Short Answer/Fill-in/True or False

6. What are the two primary functions every business performs?

7. True or False: The economy is an organic system where all parts are connected to all other parts; the opportunities to profit from these connections are limited.

8. What is the most important part of BCM? Why?

9. True or False: The staff functions are the heart of the enterprise/business?

Discussion/Essay/Assignment

10. In this chapter, Uncle Eric states that all businesses and homes have line and staff functions.

    Based on the knowledge you gained in this chapter, construct a list of both the line and staff functions of your home (or, with your parent's help, his/her business). Be sure to mention the production functions and sales functions. (Use the examples Uncle Eric provides in this chapter as a guide).

Chapter 6: The Clipper Ship Strategy

Define

1. Depression:

Short Answer/Fill-in/True or False

2. What are the four important rules for achieving success as demonstrated by the story of the extreme clipper?

Discussion/Essay/Assignment

3. In this chapter, Uncle Eric lists the four important rules for achieving success as demonstrated by the story of the extreme clipper.

   Illustrate how the clipper ships of the 1840s and 1850s followed these rules.   Be sure to list the rule first, followed by the related example from the clipper ship story.

Chapter 7: Piles of Money

Define

1. Inflation:

Short Answer/Fill-in/True or False

2. True or False: Newly created money descends on the economy in a uniform blanket.

3. True or False: The people who are first in line to get the money are able to spend it after prices rise.

4. True or False: The people who are last in line to get the money are able to spend it after prices rise.

5. Why are the people who are not early recipients of the money hurt by the situation?

Discussion/Essay/Assignment

6. To better help you visualize the concepts in this chapter, diagram/outline the events caused by cones and hot spots as discussed in this chapter.

Chapter 8: The Money Spreads

Define

1. Hyperinflation:

2. Overhead:

3. Subsidy:

4. Commodity Markets:

Short Answer/Fill-in/True or False

5. True or False: In the early stages of inflation, the money always spreads to its maximum limits rapidly.

6. In the later stages of inflation, money is very "hot" and spreads rapidly, pushing up prices quickly. If "cooling" does not occur, what will result?

7. In order to delay the onset of hyperinflation for as long as possible, governments will allow their "pitchers" (spending programs) to become_____.

Chapter 9: Cones and Sales

Define

1. Political Power:

2. Political Law:

3. Sinkholes:

Short Answer/Fill-in/True or False

4. What is one of the most effective ways for a firm to profit in a government-controlled economy?

5. What is one of the most important reasons why everyone should understand the nature and behavior of government?

6. True or False: Political law is stable and so is the flow of money.

7. The economy cannot be stable unless _____ is stable.

8. Your financial success will depend very much on your ability to answer what question?

Discussion/Essay/Assignment

9. In this chapter, Uncle Eric urges Chris to remember that a person's financial success will depend very much on his/her ability to answer the question: "Who are the buyers of my goods or services and where do they get their money?"

    Even though you probably don't sell any products/services at this stage of your life, it is never too early to begin practicing good financial strategies. This is a good exercise to work on with your teacher/parent. Select a business with which you are familiar (i.e., grocery store, bank—or your parent's business) and see if you can determine who are the buyers of their goods/services? Would they be affected by hot spots and sinkholes? How might the business owner apply the clipper ship strategy to guard against sinkholes?

Chapter 10: Scooping and Pouring

Define

1. Tax:

2. Dancing Cone:

Short Answer/Fill-in/True or False

3. True or False: All the money in "cones" is newly created.

4. The scooping process tends to leave an area economically depressed when _____.

5. Government spending frequently occurs not because someone *needs* something but because _____.

6. What must you do to be successful in a government-controlled economy?

Chapter 11: All Roads

Define

1. Demographic Hot Spots:

2. Geographic Hot Spots:

Short Answer/Fill-in/True or False

3. The Romans discovered that in a government-controlled economy no one survives unless he has _____ in the government.

4. In the United States today, what determines the location of cones?

5. In what location (city) is the most stable cone in the world?

6. What are the two types of cones (or hot spots)?

Discussion/Essay/Assignment

7. Uncle Eric gives Chris an exercise you can also try. Make two columns. Label one column: "Sources of Information on Which I Rely." List your sources. Be sure to list the exact name/ title of the source (i.e., don't list the generic term "newspaper"—list the precise name(s) of the newspaper(s) you read). Then label the adjacent column: "Government Affiliation." List how your source is affiliated to government (i.e. funding, regulations). How might an affiliation to government impact the content of your source?

For Further Reading

8. Read EVALUATING BOOKS: WHAT WOULD THOMAS JEFFERSON THINK ABOUT THIS?, an Uncle Eric book by Richard J. Maybury. This book provides key indicators and terms to help the reader learn how to identify the slants of authors, media commentators, and others. Published by Bluestocking Press, web site: www.BluestockingPress.com; Phone: 800-959-8586. For ages 12 and up.

9. Read HOW TO LIE WITH STATISTICS by Darrell Huff, published by W.W. Norton, and distributed by Bluestocking Press, web site: www.BluestockingPress.com; Phone: 800-959-8586. Excellent book. A modern classic. Shows how statistics can distort truth. For ages 14 and up.

Chapter 12: Cone Creation

Define

1. Net Tax Payers:

2. Net Tax Receivers:

3. Fiscal Policy:

4. Capitalist:

Short Answer/Fill-in/True or False

5. True or False: Foreigners, as well as Americans, court favor with U.S. politicians to change the location of the cones.

6. In Uncle Eric's opinion, do politicians corrupt capitalists, or do capitalists corrupt politicians? Provide an example to support your answer.

Chapter 13: The Super Clipper

Define

1. Super Clipper Strategy:

2. Leverage:

Short Answer/Fill-in/True or False

3. How does the Super Clipper Strategy differ from the Clipper Ship Strategy?

4. How can you gain leverage by following the strategy used by the 1840s clippers?

Discussion/Essay/Assignment

5. Go to your local library or video store and get a copy of the movie "Baby Boom" (starring Diane Keaton). As you watch the movie, keep in mind the Super Clipper Strategy (especially remember the examples Uncle Eric provides on page 77). How does Diane Keaton's character implement the Super Clipper Strategy? Is it successful for her?

Chapter 14: Do Cones Really Exist?

Short Answer/Fill-in/True or False

1. If all the money the federal government spends to fight poverty was handed directly to the poor, how much money would each family of four poor people receive per year?

2. True or False: Social-welfare programs are about helping the poor. (Be sure to support your answer.)

3. Which economic "class" (group of people) pays nearly all taxes and gets most of the subsidies?

Discussion/Essay/Assignment

4. Write a brief essay in which you explain the reasons why the government continues to fund programs to fight poverty, rather than simply giving the money spent on the programs directly to the poor. Be sure to use examples from this chapter to support your argument.

Chapter 15: The Biggest, Most Stable Cone

Define

1. Ponzi Scheme:

2. Earnings:

Short Answer/Fill-in/True or False

3. What U.S. government program is the biggest, most stable cone?

4. How is Social Security like a Ponzi (Pyramid) Scheme?

5. According to Uncle Eric, why did the U.S. government institute Social Security?

6. In what year was the idea of Social Security as an insurance program "sold" to Congress and the American public?

7. By the year 2030 how many workers will be necessary to support each Social Security recipient?

8. According to the article "How Does Social Security Affect You?" what are some of the problems created by Social Security?

Discussion/Essay/Assignment

9. In this chapter, Uncle Eric mentions that it is best to market a business in areas of the country with solid, stable economies. Large retirement communities are good examples of an area's stability. He mentions that businesses often offer senior discounts for their products/services to attract the wealth of these consumers. Look around your town and see if you can discover how businesses in your area are catering to seniors. Are there many retired/seniors in your town? How does the prosperity of your hometown correspond to other areas with more/ fewer senior residents? (U.S. Census web site might be helpful.)

10. Write a brief essay (1-2 pages) on Charles Ponzi and the concept of Ponzi Schemes.   Be sure to relate your essay to the concept of Social Security discussed in this chapter.

Chapter 16: Accidental Cones

Define

1. Deliberate Cone:

2. Malinvestment:

3. Accidental Cone:

4. Monetary Policy:

5. Regulatory Policy:

6. Invisible Hand:

7. Natural Cone:

8. Liberty:

9. Bloated Cone:

Short Answer/Fill-in/True or False

10. The New York hospitals built in 1968 to 1996 were created directly and on purpose by the government's law making, and are an example of a/an _____ Cone.

11. _____ Cones can be extremely profitable but also extremely dangerous if you do not know how to handle them.

12. In a free economy, changes in the production and distribution of wealth are organized by means of _____.

13. True or False: In a free economy, the cone/sinkhole landscape tends *not* to be very rugged. Why?

14. If you do not know whether a cone is Deliberate or Accidental, how should you classify it?

15. Is the cone/sinkhole landscape in America becoming smoother or more rugged?

16. Why do bloated cones occur?

Discussion/Essay/Assignment

17. Outline the changes in the production and distribution of wealth in a free economy and contrast that with what happens when the government intervenes.

Chapter 17: Houston: Portrait of an Accidental Cone

Define

1. Cartel:

2. Entrepreneur:

Discussion/Essay/Assignment

3. In your own words, using the example from the book, explain how Houston is an example of an Accidental Cone.

For Further Reading

4. CAPITALISM FOR KIDS by Karl Hess, published by Bluestocking Press, web site: www.BluestockingPress.com, phone: 800-959-8586. Excellent introduction to entrepreneurship for young people, ages 10 and up.

Chapter 18: Other Accidental Cones

Short Answer/Fill-in/True or False

1. True or False: Beware of the stock market because it has a tendency to become a bloated cone.

2. List the three real-life examples of Accidental Cones Uncle Eric discusses in this chapter:

3. Of the following two cones, which is the more common, and typically larger and more profitable cone, the Accidental Cone or Deliberate Cone?

4. Which cones tend to appear more quickly, Accidental Cones or Deliberate Cones?

5. How do you know when a cone is about to turn into a sinkhole?

6. Why does Uncle Eric advise young people to acquire some generalized skills/knowledge in addition to specialized skills needed for their chosen career field?

7. Which skills does Uncle Eric believe are most valuable to secure a living? Why?

Discussion/Essay/Assignment

8. Rewrite the story "Fable of the Gullible Gulls" clearly incorporating the concepts of cones/sinkholes, clippers, and other knowledge you've acquired thus far.

For Further Reading

9. UNCLE ERIC TALKS ABOUT, PERSONAL, CAREER, AND FINANCIAL SECURITY, SECOND EDITION, an Uncle Eric book by Richard J. Maybury, published by Bluestocking Press, web site: www.BluestockingPress.com, phone: 800-959-8586. Uncle Eric explains the types of knowledge, information, skills, and coursework he believes young people should study/learn in order to be prepared for the world of work, finance, and investment.

10. BUSINESS FOR KIDS: EXPLAINING COMMON SENSE REALITIES BEHIND BASIC BUSINESS PRINCIPLES by Kathryn Daniels and Anthony Joseph, published by Bluestocking Press, web site: www.BluestockingPress.com, phone: 800-959-8586. Excellent introduction to common sense business for young people ages 10 and up.

Chapter 19: Hollow Cones

Define

1. Hollow Cone:

2. Production Boom:

3. Sales Boom:

Short Answer/Fill-in/True or False

4. Why does a cone collapse?

5. What does Uncle Eric feel is perhaps the cruelest type of cone? Why?

6. Which is a safer, less-risky, investment, a *production boom* or *sales boom*. Why?

7. Many forecasts are nonsense and are dangerously misleading. Why?

8. How rapidly can a Deliberate Cone disappear? How quickly can an Accidental Cone disappear?

Discussion/Essay/Assignment

9. In your own words, describe the life cycle (based on the illustrations at the end of this chapter) for a Deliberate Cone and a Hollow Cone.

Chapter 20: An Ecosystem in Chaos

Discussion/Essay/Assignment

1. Explain in your own words, with support from the book, how the Biosphere 2 project is similar to a government-controlled economy.

Chapter 21: Outside Sales

Define

1. Outside Sales:

2. Qualify:

3. Capital:

4. Filled Cone:

5. ACF (Accidental Cone Filled):

6. ACH (Accidental Cone Hollow):

Short Answer/Fill-in/True or False

7. Accidental Cones are the cause of _____ and _____.

8. The realization that Hollow Cones exist is especially important to _____ sales people.

9. What does it mean to *qualify* your prospects on your first sales visit?

10. When you ask a businessperson the question "How's business?" what answer do you want to hear? What answer *don't* you want to hear? Why?

11. True or False: A lot of investment is done on the basis of wishful thinking; so before you get involved in a cone, look for evidence of real flows of money.

Discussion/Essay/Assignment

12. Pretend that you are an outside sales person. Using the guidelines Uncle Eric has provided in this, and previous, chapter(s), what should be your strategy for locating prospects most likely to buy from you?

Chapter 22: The Benefits of This Understanding

Define

1. Equity:

Short Answer/Fill-in/True or False

2. In this chapter, Uncle Eric advises Chris to warn friends and family about what type of cone?

3. True or False: The Employment Act of 1946, the FDIC, Federal Reserve, and other government agencies all insure that a depression cannot happen.

4. True or False: Small, localized depressions are common.

5. What is the best way to deal with small, localized depressions?

Chapter 23: Tax and Regulatory Cones

Define

1. Legislation:

Short Answer/Fill-in/True or False:

2. Geographic areas in which firms receive various tax breaks and regulatory exemptions are called _____ _____.

3. True or False: Changes in taxes and regulations confuse the market's natural steering mechanism of supply, demand, and price.

4. How do changes in taxes reshape the cone/sinkhole landscape?

Chapter 24: Marginality

Define

1. Marginality:

2. Runaway Inflation:

Short Answer/Fill-in/True or False

3. A tiny change in a tax or regulation can have an enormous effect on you due to what economic principle?

4. True or False: Any new tax or other change in political law, no matter how small, will create a sinkhole.

5. _____ is probably the most effective method of building a cone by creating thousands of little-noticed sinkholes.

Discussion/Essay/Assignment

6. Define the three main points Uncle Eric discusses in this chapter and illustrate how they relate to the story of the hamburger vendor discussed in this chapter.

Chapter 25: Marketing Managers

Define

1. Anomalies:

Short Answer/Fill-in/True or False

2. True or False: Each and every business must stay in one location and sell to people in that same location. (Provide examples to support your position.)

3. What types of careers or businesses does Uncle Eric advise Chris to enter into so that Chris will have a comfortable way to "be a clipper?" Why?

Chapter 26: The Automobile

Define

1. Commodities:

Short Answer/Fill-in/True or False

2. How does the automobile help lessen the severity of chaos and hardships produced by dancing cones?

To View or For Further Reading

3. Uncle Eric suggests you read the book THE GRAPES OF WRATH, or watch the movie to observe how farm families used their vehicles to find new cones during the Great Depression. He also suggests studying about the Transcontinental Railroad built in the 1860s, an enormous cone that sucked huge amounts of capital into the West creating boom towns all along the tracks.

Chapter 27: How to Follow the Cones

Short Answer/Fill-in/True or False

1. The successful firms of yesterday were those who sought customers with incomes that were _____. The successful firms of tomorrow will be those that seek customers with incomes that are _____.

Discussion/Essay/Assignment

2. Try to use one, or all, of the data research methods Uncle Eric suggests in this chapter to help identify cones and sinkholes (ask a reference librarian, read INFORMATION USA, or visit the Federal Reserve Economic Data web page). If you have a family member or friend who has their own business, see if you can locate information that might be helpful to them. If not, try to find data that would be interesting to you, such as identifying the cones/sinkholes in your geographic area.

Chapter 28: A Case Study: Sacramento

Discussion/Essay/Assignment

1. Uncle Eric discusses Sacramento, California, in this chapter, and remarks that the region has received a lot of federal funds over the years. How much federal funding does your state's capital region currently receive?

Chapter 29: Hot Spots and Zips

Short Answer/Fill-in/True or False

1. True or False: No matter how bad general business conditions become in the country as a whole, there are always cones somewhere.

2. The digits in a zip code are organized to focus on geographic targets around the country. What does each digit indicate?

Discussion/Essay/Assignment

3. Try to dissect your own zip code and the zip codes of your friends and family. Pay special attention to the third, forth, and fifth digits: do you share a major mailing center with any of your family and friends? What about a local mailing station? Is there much demographic or economic diversity between the regions indicated by the zip codes? How would you look at these zip codes if you were trying to market a product? What does the four-digit extension represent that completes a nine-digit zip code?

Chapter 30: The Importance of a Model for Sorting Your Data

Define

1. Gross National Product (GNP):

2. Accidental Cone Hollow (ACH):

3. Accidental Cone Filled (ACF):

Short Answer/Fill-in/True or False

4. True or False: The desperate search for information leads to economic chaos which leads to the desperate search for ways to cope.

5. How do you know which data are important and which are not?

6. The big challenge is not so much in finding data to use, but in _____.

7. BCM/The Clipper Ship Strategy provides a _____ for selecting and processing the correct data.

Discussion/Essay

8. In this chapter, Uncle Eric explains the importance of a *model* in helping us to "separate the wheat from the chaff." Explain what he means by this. Then, try consciously bearing in mind the concept of models next time you read an article or book for school. After you finish reading, write down the information you believe was most important. If you do this exercise with other students, compare your answers. Did you each write down the same things? If not, consider that perhaps you have different *models* for sorting data.   How do you, personally, decide which information is important to you? How did you form your *models* (i.e., advice from parents, friends, etc.)?

Chapter 31: Cone Classification

Discussion/Essay

1. In this chapter, Uncle Eric states the formula that entrepreneurs use to make sales:

    a. Find out exactly who the customers are.
    b. Find out exactly what they want.
    c. Find a way to acquire or produce it.
    d. Tell them you can supply it to them.
    e. Remind them of the benefits to them.
    f. Ask for the money.

    For this exercise, try to implement this formula. You may either start from scratch by using this formula for a fictional business (i.e., one you think up). Or, you may look at an existing business (i.e., supermarket, salon, mail order catalog company) and dissect them, fitting each step in the formula with the way the business operates. Also, be sure to classify the business according to its category/industry in "Sensitivity to Business Cycles."

Chapter 32: Is Pinpoint Accuracy Necessary?

Short Answer/Fill-in/True or False

1. If your firm is the type that sells high value goods or services to a small number of people, do you want to classify your customers broadly or with great individual accuracy? Why?

2. If your firm is the type that sells inexpensive items to a large number of occasional one-type customers, do you want to classify your customers broadly or with great individual accuracy? Why?

3. True or False: If you are someone's employee, you personally are a firm with one customer.

Chapter 33: How to Classify Cones

Define

1. DCF1:

2. DCF2:

3. DCF3:

4. ACF:

5. ACH:

6. S (Sinkhole):

Short Answer/Fill-in/True or False

7. For each person or firm you are trying to classify, what two questions should you ask?
   a.
   b.

8. Which is the better customer in the long run, a Deliberate Cone (DC) or an Accidental Cone Filled (ACF)? Why?

9. True or False: Your DCs are your source of stability and your ACFs are your source of large profits.

10. _____ are resistant to changes in the Federal Reserve's monetary policy and _____ are not. (Fill in the blanks with either DCs or ACs to make the statement correct.)

11. True or False: You should never target an ACF. (Explain your answer.)

12. In this chapter, Uncle Eric lists 12 classifications of cones, however, he believes most people can get by using just four categories for classification. Name these four categories.

Discussion/Essay

13. In this chapter, Uncle Eric recommends that everyone (particularly business owners or potential business owners, and those in the field of marketing) try to classify people and firms as: DC, ACF, ACH, or S. Using the definition and examples for these classifications that are provided in this chapter, try to classify your family's and friends' businesses or the businesses that employ them as DCs, ACFs, ACHs, or Ss.

Chapter 34: Precision and Size of Firm

Short Answer/Fill-in/True or False

1. In this chapter, Uncle Eric says that if you own a business, the amount of classification precision you need will depend very much on the size and type of your firm. Generally, which firm requires greater precision: a small firm or a large firm?

2. Uncle Eric says, "If you encounter a cone difficult to classify, and the expense of accumulating the additional data needed to classify it is great, always err on the side of caution." Consequently, if you do not know whether a cone is a DC or an AC, assume it is _____; if you do not know whether it is Filled or Hollow, assume it is _____. Why should you err on the side of caution in this case?

Chapter 35: Split Cones

Define

1. Split Cones (SC):

2. Accidental Cone Exporter (ACE):

3. Accidental Cone Importer (ACI):

4. Business cycle Insensitive (I):

5. Somewhat business cycle sensitive (Sw):

6. Very business cycle sensitive (V):

Short Answer/Fill-in/True or False

7. Another way to classify cones is according to their sensitivity to the business cycle. Essentially, how can the sensitivity to the business cycle be determined?

8. Provide examples of businesses that are *sensitive* to the business cycle. Contrast this with examples of businesses that are *insensitive* to business cycles.

Chapter 36: An Eerie Feeling

Assignment

1. Uncle Eric emphasizes that, by learning the classification system (i.e., DC versus AC, etc.) early in life you can test your abilities to classify accurately until you can do it as naturally as breathing. Then, when you are ready to start a career or business, you will be prepared. Keep a classification notebook/journal for at least one week. Whenever you visit a business, try to classify it and record this classification in your notebook. While reading the newspaper or watching television, try to classify the careers of the people you see/read about. For example, how would you classify your neighborhood grocery store? The auto dealership? A television news anchor? Political lobbyists?

Chapter 37: Gathering More Information

Short Answer/Fill-in/True or False

1. In this chapter, Uncle Eric mentions that many businesses have prize drawings using customers' business cards. What is the logic for doing this? What is the business gaining by using this type of product promotion?

Chapter 38: Specialized Organizations and Publications

Assignment

1. In this chapter, Uncle Eric says, "No matter what group you are trying to reach, someone else is already reaching them. No need to reinvent the wheel." He advises companies to build a carefully classified customer base by looking up associations. One way to do this is by using your phone book. Try looking up "Associations" in your Yellow Pages, and then classify each association as DC, AC, ACF, etc. What do these classifications tell you about the stability of each association? About their desirability as potential customers?

Chapter 39: External Information—A D.E.W. Line

Define

1. Distant Early Warning Line (D.E.W. Line):

2. Lobbyist:

Short Answer/Fill-in/True or False

3. Generally, what does it mean if you cannot find a newsletter or organization associated with a DC?

4. _____ is the greatest influence on any cone.

5. Many ACs either contain, or are associated with, companies large enough to have their stocks traded on the stock exchanges. This means that there are thousands of stockbrokers and mutual fund managers constantly analyzing the health of these companies and, by extension, the health of the cones. How does this work?

Assignment

6. The Federal Business Opportunities web site, designated by the Federal Acquisition Regulation, is, in effect, a listing on the Internet announcing the creation of new cones. Visit this website and explore. Write a brief synopsis of your findings. (At time of publication, the web address is: www.fedbizopps.gov)

Chapter 40: S.I.C. Codes

Define

1. S.I.C. codes (Standard Industrial Classification codes):

2. House Organ:

Assignment

3. In this chapter, Uncle Eric advises: "Know thy cones." He states that each area of the country has a different mix of industries and occupations. What industries and occupations do your city, county, and state specialize in?

Chapter 41: List Companies and Marketing Data

Short Answer/Fill-in/True or False

1. In this chapter, Uncle Eric talks about the DIRECT MAIL LIST CATALOG. What is this catalog and what is its function? How can a businessperson use it relative to the concept of cones?

Chapter 42: Importance of Real Estate

Short Answer/Fill-in/True or False

1. True or False: Real estate is the best indicator of the location of cones and sinkholes. Support your answer.

2. Using the terms *sinkhole* or *cone*, correctly complete the following: "Where property values are skyrocketing you will find a _____, and where they are falling you will find a _____."

Chapter 43: Learn by Example

Short Answer/Fill-in/True or False

1. In this chapter, Uncle Eric suggests that we should learn from the example of others. What example can we learn from Creel Morell Inc.?

Chapter 44: Sales Side Summary

Short Answer/Fill-in/True or False

1. BCM is divided into sales strategies and production strategies. What are the five main points (summary) of the sales strategy?

Part 2: Production Strategy

Chapter 45: Stomping the Town

Short Answer/Fill-in/True or False

1. Relate the concepts of Godzilla and political law. How is one to cope in areas where the threat of "Godzilla" is present?

Chapter 46: Your Factors of Production

Define

1. Factors of Production:

2. Land:

3. Labor:

4. Capital:

5. Entrepreneur:

Short Answer/Fill-in/True or False

6. Of the four factors of production, which does Uncle Eric believe is most important? Why?

For Further Reading

7. Read CAPITALISM FOR KIDS by Karl Hess, published by Bluestocking Press, web site: www.BluestockingPress.com, phone: 530-622-8586 or 800-959-8586. Highly recommended. Hess does an excellent job of explaining the philosophy of entrepreneurship and includes a self-test to determine if the reader has the personality and temperament to be an entrepreneur. For ages 12 and up.

Chapter 47: Streamlining

Define

1. Streamlined:

Short Answer/Fill-in/True or False

2. To minimize risks and maximize profits in an environment of political law, you must be highly adaptable. What does this mean?

3. Ideally, in a government-controlled economy a firm should consist only of

   _____

4. Ideally, what are the only two roles the entrepreneur should perform?

5. True or False: In a land controlled by political law, the three keys to success are: mobility, mobility, and mobility.

Chapter 48: Cyclical Problems

Short Answer/Fill-in/True or False

1. When the economy is expanding, production is the major problem. According to Uncle Eric, why is this the case?

2. When the economy experiences a bust, marketing becomes the problem. According to Uncle Eric, why is this the case?

3. True or False: Bankruptcies are made during busts, not booms.

Chapter 49: Break-Even Analysis

Define

1. Break-Even Analysis:

2. Fixed Costs:

3. Variable Costs:

4. Rent:

5. Break-Even Point:

Short Answer/Fill-in/True or False

6. Look at your house, not just the building itself, but the items it contains and the services that make it run. Make a list of what is a "fixed cost" and what is a "variable cost." Try to be as detailed as possible. For example: A table lamp is a fixed cost. It has already been purchased—no matter whether you turn on the lamp once a day or once a year, the cost of the lamp stays the same. Electricity, however, is a variable cost—the amount of money you pay for electricity will vary depending on how often you turn on the lamp.

Chapter 50: Mrs. Garcia

Define

1. Fascism:

Short Answer/Fill-in/True or False

2. According to "Mrs. Garcia," Panama's laws changed constantly and one never knew what the government would do next. This great uncertainty created great risk for anyone investing hard-earned money in Panama. Consequently, where did most Panamanians keep their money? How did an owner of Panamanian plant/equipment protect his/her holdings from burdensome taxes, regulations, or confiscation?

3. What is the lesson that "Mrs. Garcia" taught Uncle Eric?

Chapter 51: A New Industry

Define

1. De-industrialization:

Short Answer/Fill-in/True or False

2. "A good rule of thumb: If it cannot be easily sold at a good price during the next recession _____."

3. "A better rule: Determine exactly what service it performs for you, then _____."

4. Uncle Eric says that an offshoot of de-industrialization is employee-leasing. What is employee-leasing?

5. True or False: De-industrialization is caused by the existence of political law.

Assignment

6. Visit the library and ask a librarian for a copy of one of the articles Uncle Eric recommends in this chapter. What did you learn from the article? How do the concepts/examples presented in the article relate to what you have learned in THE CLIPPER SHIP STRATEGY?

Chapter 52: Break-Even Solutions

Define

1. Break-Even Flexibility:

2. Payback Analysis:

Short Answer/Fill-in/True or False

3. In this chapter, Uncle Eric outlines three ways to solve break-even problems. What are they?

4. What is the benefit of renting versus owning a business building or home?

5. Uncle Eric says that if you must use debt financing in a business, use it only for variable costs. Why?

6. Why should you not get involved in any project that will take more than a year to go all the way to completion?

Chapter 53: The Most Risky Investment

Short Answer/Fill-in/True or False

1. According to Uncle Eric, what is the most risky investment? Why?

Chapter 54: Specialization

Define

1. Specialization of Labor:

2. Scientific Law:

Short Answer/Fill-in/True or False

3. In an environment of political law, the big dollars are earned by the _____, not the _____.

Chapter 55: Payback Analysis

Short Answer/Fill-in/True or False

1. Uncle Eric states that one of the most helpful concepts to understand is payback analysis. Define "payback."

2. True or False: The higher the payback percentage the higher the risk.

3. In a business, generally do earlier investments or later investments have a better payback?

Chapter 56: Start-Up Firms: An Example

Short Answer/Fill-in/True or False

1. What is the difference between the "Horatio Alger" tradition of starting the Yummy Gobblies cereal company and the BCM model for starting the Yummy Gobblies cereal company?

Chapter 57: Careers in BCM

Short Answer/Fill-in/True or False

1. In this chapter, Uncle Eric recommends that Chris should start a BCM consulting firm. Why does Uncle Eric recommend this?

Chapter 58: Investment Strategy

Short Answer/Fill-in/True or False

1. What does Uncle Eric say about long-term investment plans?

2. What is the purpose of savings?

3. According to Uncle Eric, when should you commit funds that you earmarked for speculation?

4. True or False: Uncle Eric says to always be diversified, never put all your eggs in one basket.

Chapter 59: Two Types of Investment Cones

Define

1. Double Cone Investment:

2. Capital Gain:

3. Single Cone Investments:

Short Answer/Fill-in/True or False

4. What lesson can be learned from financier Baron Rothschild?

Chapter 60: Summary

Final Assignment

1. In this final chapter, Uncle Eric urges Chris to "Be a Clipper!" and to share the lessons of BCM with the people Chris cares about. Now that you have finished THE CLIPPER SHIP STRATEGY it is your turn to share your knowledge with others. Write a letter to a friend, family member, or teacher (or all the people you care about) sharing with them the lessons you've learned from this book. Remember to cover all eight of Uncle Eric's summary points from this chapter, and be sure to emphasize that BCM should be used only to tap into cones that already exist—it is unethical to do something to *create* a Deliberate Cone. Spread the word and "Be a Clipper!"

Final Exam

1. What is the business cycle?

2. What is Business Cycle Management (BCM):

3. What is the difference between wealth and money?

4. Explain the concept of a model as applied by Uncle Eric. How do models help us?

5. What is the discount rate and how is it used by the Federal Reserve?

6. How does one arrive at the "real" money supply?

7. What is the difference between evidence and forecasts as applicable to business situations?

8. Of the three schools of economics (Austrian, Keynesian, Monetarists), which has the most free market economic viewpoint today?

9. What makes Austrian economics different from other schools of economics?

10. Explain: line, staff, production, and sales functions.

11. What is the Clipper Ship Strategy (not the book, but the strategy)?

12. What are the two primary functions every business performs?

13. What are the four important rules for achieving success as demonstrated by the story of the extreme clipper?

14. Why are the people who are not early recipients of the money that is injected into the economy hurt by the situation?

15. True or False: In the early stages of inflation, the money always spreads to its maximum limits rapidly.

16. True or False: Political law is stable and so is the flow of money.

17. True or False: The economy cannot be stable unless law is stable.

18. True or False: All the money in "cones" is newly created. Explain.

19. In the United States today, what determines the location of cones?

20. What location (city) is the most stable cone in the world?

21. What is a Ponzi Scheme?

22. What U.S. government program is the biggest, most stable cone?

23. In what year was the idea of Social Security as an insurance program "sold" to Congress and the American public?

24. What are some of the problems created by Social Security?

25. What is a Deliberate Cone?

26. What is an Accidental Cone?

27. What is a Natural Cone?

28. True or False: Accidental Cones can be extremely profitable but also extremely dangerous if you do not know how to handle them.

29. In a free economy, the cone/sinkhole landscape tends *not* to be very rugged. Why?

30. What is an entrepreneur and what does an entrepreneur do?

31. Of the following two cones, which is the more common, and typically larger, and more profitable cone, the Accidental Cone or Deliberate Cone?

32. How do you know when a cone is about to turn into a sinkhole?

33. Which is a safer, less-risky, investment, a *production boom* or *sales boom*. Why?

34. Define "capital."

35. Accidental Cones are the cause of _____ and _____.

36. True or False: Changes in taxes and regulations confuse the market's natural steering mechanism of supply, demand, and price.

37. True or False: Inflation is probably the most effective method of building a cone by creating thousands of little-noticed sinkholes.

38. True or False: No matter how bad general business conditions become in the country as a whole, there are always cones somewhere.

39. Define "Gross National Product."

40. How do you know which data are important and which are not?

41. True or False: If you are someone's employee, you personally are a firm with one customer.

42. Which is the better customer in the long run, a Deliberate Cone (DC) or an Accidental Cone Filled (ACF)? Why?

43. _____ _____ is the greatest influence on any cone.

44. True or False: Real estate is the best indicator of the location of cones and sinkholes.

45. According to Uncle Eric, "Where property values are skyrocketing you will find a _____, and where they are falling you will find a _____."

46. The four factors of production are _____, _____, _____, and _____.

47. Of the four factors of production, which does Uncle Eric believe is most important? Why?

48. To minimize risks and maximize profits in an environment of political law, you must be highly adaptable. What does this mean?

49. True or False: In a land controlled by political law, the three keys to success are: mobility, mobility, and mobility.

50. Define: Break-Even Point

51. Define: De-industrialization

52. According to Uncle Eric, what is the most risky investment? Why?

53. In an environment of political law, the big dollars are earned by the _____, not the _____.

54. True or False: The higher the payback percentage the higher the risk. Why?

55. According to Uncle Eric, when should you commit funds that you earmarked for speculation?

Thought Exercises Revisited (This can be an oral or written exercise.)

56. Before you began to read THE CLIPPER SHIP STRATEGY you were asked to answer the Thought Exercises on page 11 of this Study Guide. Now that you have finished reading THE CLIPPER SHIP STRATEGY, review your answers to the Thought Exercises. Would you make any changes to your answers? Explain what changes you would make and why. If you would make no changes, explain why you are satisfied with your answers as previously written. If you did not originally provide an answer for lack of knowledge, answer the exercises now.

Answers

Uncle Eric's Model of How the World Works

Short Answer/Fill-in/True or False

1. Uncle Eric says that models are how we think. They are how we understand how the world works.

2. According to Uncle Eric, models are important because we constantly refer to our models to help us determine what incoming data is important and what data is not.

3. It is important to sort incoming data because we need to decide what incoming data we need to remember or file for future reference, and what data we can discard, based on its importance to us, or its usefulness. We need a tool for making this determination. That tool is also called our "model."

4. This answer requires the student to draw his/her own conclusion based on the information provided in the explanation of "Uncle Eric's Model of How the World Works." Possible answer: We should always be willing to test our models against incoming data, and if our models don't stand up to the incoming data, then it becomes necessary to question and perhaps rethink our model, as well as question the reliability of the incoming data.

5. Free market economics and Higher Law are the two models Uncle Eric thinks are most reliable, as well as crucially important for everyone to learn. Free market economics and Higher Law are important models because they show how human civilization works, especially the world of money.

6. **Fascism** is the political philosophy that is no philosophy at all. It embraces the concept that those in power can do whatever appears necessary to achieve their goals.

Discussion/Essay/Assignment

7. Examples of models will vary and might include scientific models, religious models, economic models, political models, etc.

8. The book THE CLIPPER SHIP STRATEGY explains how government's involvement in the economy affects business, careers, and investments. Not always knowing what government's going to do next, this book provides practical strategy for prospering in a turbulent economy.

9. Answers will vary.

10. Look at the front matter of your dictionary. There should be an explanation of the "Order of Definitions." For example, the order of definitions can be historical order: the earliest meaning is placed first and later meanings are arranged by semantic development.

11. The reader must understand what the author means by the words the author uses so the reader can understand the progression of the author's ideas that build on the definition of the terms used. This does not require that a reader agree with the author's definition of a word, only that the reader understand what the author means when the author uses the word. Then the reader is in a better position to critically examine the author's ideas based on a common understanding of the author's meaning.

12. Answers will vary, but might include some of the following explanations: Definitions provide clear understanding and communication between the parties involved. For example, suppose you eat a piece of fruit. This fruit happens to be a banana. Someone comes along who has never before seen or tasted a banana. With the banana in your presence, you can each begin to discuss its merits, and you will each know exactly what you're talking about. As in the Richard Feynman example, you are understanding the characteristics of the banana that go into making up what that "thing" is. To be able to give the "thing" a name, banana, that both parties can use in future communication will help promote speedier and clearer communication. This is the purpose of always making sure that you understand the definition of a term used in a discussion (whether in conversation or in books). You don't have to agree with the person's definition, but if you understand what the person means by it, you can have a clearer and more meaningful discussion instead of getting bogged down in misunderstandings regarding fuzzy language.

Author's Disclosure

Short Answer/Fill-in/True or False

1. Juris Naturalism is the belief in a Natural Law that is higher than any government's law.

Discussion/Essay/Assignment

2. Answers will vary, but students should note that the bias or philosophical slant of an author, news commentator, or reporter can influence the selection of facts included in a book or report, thereby slanting the history, or other subject areas.

3. Answers will vary.
4. Answers will vary.
5. Answers will vary.
6. Answers will vary.

Thought Exercises

1-4. Answers will vary, but should show thought and logic.

5. One of the safest geographical locations to start a business or look for a job might be Washington D.C. or a state capitol since government monies are more stable to these areas.

Part 1: Sales Strategy

Chapter 1: A Strategy for Success

Define

1. Economics. The study of the production and distribution of wealth.

2. Business Cycle Management (BCM). An investment strategy that shows business managers and sales people how to take advantage of the fact that pockets of prosperity can be discovered and tapped into, no matter how good or bad business conditions may be.

3. Recession. The beginning of a depression that never went all the way.

4. Economy. Statists and other powerseekers see the economy as a kind of machine that can be adjusted or "fine tuned." In reality, the economy is a kind of ecology made of biological organisms—humans. Trying to fine tune or adjust them tends to damage them.

5. Boom-and-Bust Cycle. The so-called business cycle. The pattern of inflationary economic expansions alternating with deflationary contractions (recessions and depressions).

6. Injection Effect. The change that occurs on Wall Street (the financial world) and Main Street (where most of us live and work) when the government injects new money into the economy.

7. Business Cycle. The "boom-and-bust" cycle of inflationary expansions and deflationary contractions or recessions.

8. Money Supply. The amount of money in an economy.

9. Velocity. The speed at which money changes hands.

10. Money Demand. The desire to own money.

11. Theory. Coherent set of ideas that seem to explain a reality.

12. Application. Practice in the real world.

13. Statist. One who believes in government as the solution to problems. Statists assume the benefits of government activities can be greater than total costs.

14. Laws. Broadly speaking, the rules for human conduct that are enforced by violence or threats of violence. More narrowly, law sometimes means common law or natural law, as distinct from legislation. "A nation of laws and not of men" means a nation in which the highest law is Common Law or Natural Law, not legislation.

Short Answer/Fill-in/True or False

15. The *Flying Cloud* was a clipper ship, built in 1851, which traveled from New York to San Francisco, around Cape Horn, in a record 89 days.

16. True. In bad times as well as good, someone is always earning money. Even during the Great Depression, when most people were barely able to survive, some people were getting rich.

17. It is important to start incorporating the BCM model into the daily way of looking at the world because people will be in a better position to protect themselves from the boom-and-bust business cycle and to benefit from the injection effect in adulthood.

Discussion/Essay/Assignment

18. Answers will vary. Save your response, you will be asked to revisit this question.

Chapter 2: Ethics and the Flood of Data

Define

1. Zero Sum Game. An activity in which one person can win only if another person loses.

2. Wealth. Goods and services—food, clothing, haircuts, cars, TVs, homes, and everything else that makes life better. Not to be confused with money. Money can be wealth, but it is only one kind.

3. Money. The most easily traded thing in a society. Economists call it the most liquid commodity. Money is the tool we use to measure and trade wealth.

4. Model. A mental picture of how the world works. Models are how we think; models are how we understand how the world works.

Short Answer/Fill-in/True or False

5. The first two important points in the discussion of BCM are: a) **The ethics of BCM**, and b) **the deluge of business information that threatens to engulf us today**.

6. When considering the ethics of BCM and the injection effect, you must remember that the injection effect is wrong and hurts millions of people. If you are ever in a position to stop the government's injection of money, you should do so. However, if you do not have control over the injections it is not wrong to profit from them: there is nothing wrong with becoming more prosperous as long as you are not harming someone else. (Also, remember to tell your friends and family about BCM and the injection effect so that they can benefit from the knowledge, too.)

7. Wealth is goods and services; money is the tool we use to measure and trade wealth. As long as a person has wealth, money is a minor consideration.

8. The economy is *not* a zero sum game. The amount of wealth can be increased so one person can have more without another having less.

9. Models help us sort and prioritize information—they help us know what information is important and what information is not.

Discussion/Essay/Assignment

10. Answers will vary, but the effort of applying models to daily experiences should demonstrate that the student understands the concept of "model."

Chapter 3: Hot Spots and Evidence

Define

1. "Real" Money Supply. Subtract price increases from money supply increases to get the "real" money supply.

2. The Federal Reserve (the Fed). The central bank of the U.S.

3. Discount Rate. The discount rate is an interest rate and one of the Federal Reserve's tools for manipulating the money supply. A rising rate means a restricted money supply, and a falling rate means a rising money supply.

4. Hot Spots. Demographic or geographic areas where new money is injected. These points of injection offer business, career, and investment opportunities.

5. Evidence. Facts that tend to verify.

6. Forecasts. Predictions based on analysis of available data.

7. Shares of Stock. Certificates of ownership in a corporation.

8. Standards of Proof. Measures of authenticity.

9. Price. An exchange rate.

10. Bull Market. A strongly rising market. Opposite of a bear market.

11. Bear Market. A falling market. Opposite of a bull market.

Short Answer/Fill-in/True or False

12. Money does not descend on the economy in a uniform blanket. Instead, it is injected into specific locations, as directed by the government, and spreads outward *unevenly* from those locations. Consequently, some areas are flooded with new money while others receive none.

13. No, hot spots do not remain constant. Spots that were hot in the past may not be hot in the future—no hot spot lasts forever.

14. A forecast is a *prediction based on analysis of available data.* Evidence is *facts that tend to verify.* In his example about purchasing shares in XYZ company, Uncle Eric demonstrates that, when looking at a business situation, you should always demand *evidence.* (i.e., If a business claims to have entered a profitable hot spot and shows you "proof" in the form of new buildings and employee expansion, this is *not* evidence. The company is simply *forecasting* that they will profit from the hot spot. Proof that the company's sales have expanded will provide *evidence* that they have tapped into the money from the hot spot).

15. True. When lots of people who know nothing about something are buying it, that is a good time to sell it because usually the last people to get into an investment are those who know nothing about it; once they are in, there is no one else left to buy it so the price cannot go much higher.

Discussion/Essay/Assignment

16. The major economic events of the period from 1970 to 1990 include:

1970: Real money supply is $1400 billion.

Fed begins increasing the money supply to end the 1982 recession. The supply of dollars increased, and the value of each dollar fell.

1986: International investors have begun losing confidence in the stability of the U.S. dollar. Many no longer wanted it, so its value in international currency markets was falling.

1987: To protect the dollar, the Fed begins restricting the growth of the money supply. (This triggered the 1987 stock market crash and, later, the 1990 recession.)

1990: Real money supply is $2500 billion. Recession begins.

1991: The recession becomes a political issue. President Bush's job approval rate is falling. Fed under pressure to re-inflate the U.S. into an economic boom before the 1992 elections.

1992: On December 20th, Fed cut the discount rate a full 3.5%, signaling that re-inflation had begun. The stock market shot upward.

From 1992 to 1997: The money supply increased $425 billion and the stock market rose more than 100%.

Chapter 4: Austrian Economics

Define

1. Cold Spot. An area where sales are slack and incomes are low. An area of depressed economic activity.

2. Austrian Economics. The most free-market of all the economic viewpoints today. The origin was in Vienna, Austria, but the country where it is most popular today is probably the U.S. Austrian economists have won Nobel Prizes, and the most widely known Austrian economist, F.A. Hayek, was highly influential in the economic policies of British Prime Minister Margaret Thatcher. Austrian economics sees the economy not as a machine, but as an almost infinitely complex ecology made of biological organisms — humans.

3. Keynesian Economics. Originally the economic philosophy of economist John Maynard Keynes. Today a kind of compromise, or middle road, between socialism and capitalism. Keynesians want broad government controls on economic activity, especially manipulation of the money supply. "Keynesian" is sometimes used as a synonym for "inflationist," or one who advocates inflating the money supply.

4. Monetarist Economics. A free-market economic philosophy. Focuses on increases in money supply causing rising prices. Associated with the economics department of the University of Chicago; monetarism is sometimes called the Chicago school of economics.

5. Cones. An area where money is flowing in large quantities and firms are placing plant and equipment to tap into these flows.

6. Ecology. As it relates to the economy, the highly complex interrelationships among people.

Short Answer/Fill-in/True or False

7. The examples in Uncle Eric's letters are drawn mostly from the period 1970 to 1990 because these decades contained three full economic cycles, including the worst recession since the Great Depression. We are now far enough removed from those events so that we can study them with the clarity of hindsight.

8. Few of today's business people have studied the concepts of free-market Austrian economics. Most have studied Keynesian or Monetarist economics because the U.S. government uses Keynesian and Monetarist economics, so this is what is taught in most colleges.

9. One of the strengths in Monetarist economics is its teachings about the subject of *velocity*.

10. One of the weaknesses in Austrian economics as well as other economic models is that they were created by theoreticians who were trying to understand how the world works, but had little interest in practical applications for people to use in daily life.

11. Most economists from schools other than Austrian economics assume that the economy is a giant machine. Austrian economists see the economy not as a machine but as an *ecology* since it is made up of organisms—people.

12. True. Free-market "Austrian" economics is the only type of economics that has done a thorough investigation of the injection effect.

Discussion/Essay/Assignment

13. Answers will vary.
14. Answers will vary.

Chapter 5: Line and Staff

Define

1. Line Functions. Sales and production.

2. Staff Functions. Support for the line function that includes accounting, finance, legal, personnel, administration, etc.

3. Production Function. Parts of a firm that create the goods or services.

4. Sales Function. The activity of trading a firm's goods or services for money.

5. Clipper Ship Strategy. A tool for discovering where there is a pile of money. The Clipper Ship Strategy advocates tapping into that pile of money and always to be searching for new piles because no pile lasts forever.

Short Answer/Fill-in/True or False

6. Sales and Production are the two primary functions every business performs.

7. False. The economy is an organic system where all parts are connected to all other parts; the opportunities to profit from these connections are limitless.

8. The most important part of BCM is the *Clipper Ship Strategy*. It allows you to learn from history, profit by what you know, or, at the very least, minimize your chances of being economically hurt.

9. False. The *line* functions are the heart of the home and business enterprise.

Discussion/Essay/Assignment

10. Answers will vary.

Chapter 6: The Clipper Ship Strategy

Define

1. Depression. The correction period following an inflation. Usually includes a lot of business failures and unemployment.

Short Answer/Fill-in/True or False

2. The four important rules for achieving success as demonstrated by the story of the extreme clipper are: 1) Find out where there is a pile of money; 2) Tap into that pile; 3) Don't expect the pile to last forever; 4) Always be searching for new piles.

Discussion/Essay/Assignment

3. Answers will vary, but should be similar to the following:

    a. Find out where there is a pile of money: People on the east coast realized that profits were high on the west coast and low on the east coast.

    b. Tap into that pile: Money could be earned by quickly transporting cargo from the east coast to the west coast (where goods were in scarce supply, but money was plentiful).

    c. Don't expect it to last forever: Ship owners realized that the "hot spot" on the west coast would not last forever. They knew that whatever was done to tap into the flow would have to be done quickly (hence the speedy clipper ships).

    d. Always be searching for new piles: When the California gold rush began to wane in 1851, a new gold rush began in Australia. The clipper ships diverted from their San Francisco routes and rushed to Australia to tap into the new "hot spot" there.

Chapter 7: Piles of Money

Define

1. Inflation. An increase in the amount of money. Causes the money to lose value, so prices rise.

Short Answer/Fill-in/True or False

2. False. Newly created money does *not* descend on the economy in a uniform blanket and the belief that it does can lead to all sorts of disastrous business, career, and investment decisions.

3. False. The people who are first in line to get the money are able to spend it *before* prices rise.

4. True. The people who are last in line to get the money are able to spend it after prices rise.

5. People who are not early recipients of the money are hurt by the situation because their incomes do not rise as quickly as prices rise.

Discussion/Essay/Assignment

6. Efforts will vary based on student's level of understanding.

Chapter 8: The Money Spreads

Define

1. Hyperinflation. Runaway inflation.

2. Overhead. Overhead is a rather nebulous term that generally refers to costs that are not directly attributable to the product and are not easily cut back. Opposite of variable cost. In automobile production, steel is a variable cost, and the fire insurance on the factory is overhead.

3. Subsidy. Money given to a person or organization that did not earn it.

4. Commodity Markets. Where raw materials are bought and sold.

Short Answer/Fill-in/True or False

5. False. In the early stages of inflation, it usually takes the money a long time, sometimes years, to spread to its maximum limits.

6. In the later stages of inflation, money is very "hot" and spreads rapidly, pushing up prices quickly. If "cooling" does not occur, hyperinflation will result.

7. In order to delay the onset of hyperinflation for as long as possible, governments will allow their "pitchers" (spending programs) to become **empty.**

Chapter 9: Cones and Sales

Define

1. Political Power. The privilege of using legal force on persons who have not harmed anyone. The legal privilege of backing one's decisions with violence or threats of violence, or the legal privilege of encroaching on the life, liberty, or property of a person who has not harmed anyone.

2. Political Law. Made-up law. Same as legislation. Human law. Might makes right.

3. Sinkholes. A depressed area. An area from which more wealth is removed than is poured back in.

Short Answer/Fill-in/True or False

4. One of the most effective ways for a firm to profit in a government-controlled economy is to locate one of the pitchers of money and place itself directly beneath that pitcher.

5. Everyone should understand the nature and behavior of government because government is the most important force affecting a person's wallet — it is more important than customers, employees, *anything*.

6. False. Political law can change at any time without warning, which means that the flow of money can also change without warning.

7. The economy cannot be stable unless **law** is stable.

8. Financial success will depend on one's ability to answer this question: "Who are the buyers of my goods or services and where do they get their money?"

Discussion/Essay/Assignment

9. Answers will vary.

Chapter 10: Scooping and Pouring

Define

1. Tax. The way governments get money. To tax means to take money away from someone, by force if necessary, even if the person thinks what he is getting in return has little or no value.

2. Dancing Cone. A cone that moves to another location.

Short Answer/Fill-in/True or False

3. False. Most of the money in "cones" is old money that has been in the economy for a long time. Then the government scoops it out, in the form of tax collections, and mixes it with newly created money.

4. The scooping process tends to leave an area economically depressed when more money is scooped out of that area than is poured back in.

5. Government spending frequently occurs not because someone *needs* something but because **someone wants a cone of money created over him that will benefit him**.

6. To be successful in a government-controlled economy you must follow the dancing cones.

Chapter 11: All Roads

Define

1. Demographic Hot Spots. An identifiable group of individuals who have a lot of money to spend.

2. Geographic Hot Spots. Areas (states, counties, cities, or neighborhoods) that receive large sums of money.

Short Answer/Fill-in/True or False

3. The Romans discovered that in a government-controlled economy no one survives unless he has **connections** in the government.

4. In the United States today, political law determines the location of cones.

5. Washington D.C. is the most stable cone in the world.

6. The two types of cones (or hot spots) are: demographic and geographic.

Discussion/Essay/Assignment

7. Answers will vary.

Chapter 12: Cone Creation

Define

1. Net Tax Payers. People who pay more to the government than they get from the government.

2. Net Tax Receivers. People who get more from the government than they pay to the government.

3. Fiscal Policy. The government's spending practices.

4. Capitalist. One who believes in capitalism (free markets, free trade, and free enterprise).

Short Answer/Fill-in/True or False

5. True. Foreigners, as well as Americans, court favor with U.S. politicians to change the location of the cones.

6. In Uncle Eric's opinion, politicians corrupt capitalists. Examples may vary; Uncle Eric uses the railroads.

Chapter 13: The Super Clipper

Define

1. Super Clipper Strategy. Buying from sinkholes and selling to cones.

2. Leverage. Money borrowed for a business venture or investment.

Short Answer/Fill-in/True or False

3. The Super Clipper Strategy is more difficult to implement but even more profitable than the Clipper Ship Strategy.

4. You can gain leverage by following the strategy used by the 1840s clippers by finding depressed areas where people are willing to work cheap—then become the pipeline that links them with a cone.

Discussion/Essay/Assignment

5. Diane Keaton's character identifies a demographic group of young affluent city parents who can afford to purchase gourmet baby food which can be produced in the country where costs are less expensive.

Chapter 14: Do Cones Really Exist?

Short Answer/Fill-in/True or False

1. If all the money the federal government spends to fight poverty was handed directly to the poor, each family of four poor people would receive more than $70,000 per year in Federal money, tax free. If state and local money were included, the figure would climb to over $80,000 per year.

2. False. Social-welfare programs are not about helping the poor. According to THE ECONOMIST MAGAZINE, more than 85% of all benefits go to middle and upper classes; households with incomes above $100,000 get slightly more federal money each year than those earning one tenth of that.

3. The economic "class" (group of people) that pays nearly all taxes and gets most of the subsidies are the middle class and wealthy.

Discussion/Essay/Assignment

4. Answers will vary.

Chapter 15: The Biggest, Most Stable Cone

Define

1. Ponzi Scheme. Named after swindler Charles Ponzi, a Ponzi scheme is one in which investors are paid not from income earned by the investment but from the contributions of new investors. Ponzis go broke when the number of new investors is no longer great enough to support the earlier investors. This is also called a pyramid scheme.

2. Earnings. Income.

Short Answer/Fill-in/True or False

3. The U.S. government's Social Security program is the biggest, most stable cone.

4. Social Security is like a Ponzi (Pyramid) Scheme because the winners in Social Security are the original investors; the losers are the new investors.

5. According to Uncle Eric, the U.S. government instituted Social Security to "buy" the votes of older persons by using money taken from their sons and daughters.

6. The idea of Social Security as an insurance program was "sold" to Congress and the American public in 1935.

7. By the year 2030 two workers will be necessary to support each Social Security recipient.

8. Answers will vary, but should include such concepts such as: Social Security does not *produce* income, it only *transfers* income; Social Security does not create factories or office buildings or jobs for the young; Social Security actually *erases* jobs for the young, and contributes to the difficulty young people have in getting ahead; when someone today spends Social Security money, he/she is consuming not only his/her children's tax money, but their jobs, too.

Discussion/Essay/Assignment

9. Answers will vary.

10. Answers will vary.

Chapter 16: Accidental Cones

Define

1. Deliberate Cone. A cone created directly by government agencies injecting money into the economy in specific planned locations.

2. Malinvestment. Investment that should not have happened.

3. Accidental Cone. A cone produced accidentally by the government's fiscal, monetary, or regulatory policies.

4. Monetary Policy. The government's behavior in increasing or decreasing the supply of money.

5. Regulatory Policy. The government's behavior in trying to control our work, our property, and our investments.

6. Invisible Hand. A term coined by Adam Smith to refer to the automatic way free markets organize production according to price signals.

7. Natural Cone. An area in which the supply of money is increasing due to normal increases in demand for a good or service, not due to injections of money by the government.

8. Liberty. Protection of the individual's right to his or her life, freedom, and property. Widespread obedience to the two fundamental laws that make civilization possible: (1) Do all you have agreed to do, and (2) do not encroach on other persons or their property.

9. Bloated Cone. A cone so packed with money that it contains a huge amount of malinvestment.

Short Answer/Fill-in/True or False

10. The New York hospitals built in 1968 to 1996 were created directly and on purpose by the government's law making, and are an example of a **Deliberate** Cone.

11. **Accidental** Cones can be extremely profitable but also extremely dangerous if you do not know how to handle them.

12. In a free economy, changes in the production and distribution of wealth are organized by means of **the pricing mechanism–the so-called *invisible hand.***

13. True. In a free economy, the cone/sinkhole landscape tends *not* to be very rugged because the invisible hand works to smooth them out before they get very large.

14. If you do not know whether a cone is Deliberate or Accidental, it should be classified as an *Accidental* Cone.

15. The cone/sinkhole landscape in America is becoming more rugged.

16. Bloated cones occur because they are an *accidental* side effect of money supply expansion.

Discussion/Essay/Assignment

17. Outlines may vary.

Chapter 17: Houston: Portrait of an Accidental Cone

Define

1. Cartel. Independent commercial enterprises that combine for the purpose of limiting competition.

2. Entrepreneur. The spark plug that makes the economy run. The person who searches for opportunities, takes risks, makes the important decisions, and organizes land, labor, and capital. The essence of the firm.

Discussion/Essay/Assignment

3. Writing styles may vary, but should encompass the main points of the Houston example explained in this chapter.

Chapter 18: Other Accidental Cones

Short Answer/Fill-in/True or False

1. True. Beware of the stock market because it has a tendency to become a bloated cone.

2. The three real-life examples of Accidental Cones discussed in this chapter are: The stock market, 1970s real estate, the electronics industry.

3. Accidental Cones are more common, and typically larger and more profitable than Deliberate Cones.

4. Accidental Cones tend to appear more quickly than Deliberate Cones.

5. When a firm's sales start dropping it is a sign the flow of money might be slowing, so be cautious because a cone may be about to turn into a sinkhole.

6. Uncle Eric advises young people to acquire some generalized skills/knowledge in addition to the specialized skills needed for their chosen career field so that they will be versatile in a changing job market and better able to "sail away" (like the clippers) to new, more lucrative careers if those in their current profession turn to sinkholes.

7. Uncle Eric believes good selling skills are most valuable to secure a living because there is always a need for someone who is good at bringing buyers and sellers together.

Discussion/Essay/Assignment

8. Stories will vary.

Chapter 19: Hollow Cones

Define

1. Hollow Cone. One with plant, equipment, and workers, but little money.

2. Production Boom. Large expansion of production facilities.

3. Sales Boom. Large expansion of sales.

Short Answer/Fill-in/True or False

4. A cone collapses because it becomes hollow.

5. According to Uncle Eric the cruelest type of cone is the Accidental Cone stocked with plant and equipment in the *expectation* that a flow of money will soon develop; if the flow of money never arrives, the cone will collapse leaving the area economically devastated.

6. A sales boom is a safer, less-risky investment because it is caused by a real flow of money.

7. Many forecasts are nonsense and are dangerously misleading because they are based on the assumption that the government's behavior is predictable — but government officials *change their minds* and their cone-creating policies are in a constant state of flux.

8. A Deliberate Cone can dry up in a matter of months; an Accidental Cone can vanish within days.

Discussion/Essay/Assignment

9. Explanations will vary but should include the steps included in the illustrations at the end of this chapter.

Chapter 20: An Ecosystem in Chaos

Discussion/Essay/Assignment

1. Explanations will vary.

Chapter 21: Outside Sales

Define

1. Outside Sales. Sales that occur in the field, at the customer's office, home, or job site.

2. Qualify. Making sure a possible customer is able to pay for the purchase.

3. Capital. The buildings, office equipment, and other tools workers need to produce what we want to buy; or, the money saved to buy these things.

4. Filled Cone. A cone that has lots of money running through it.

5. ACF (Accidental Cone Filled). A cone produced accidentally by the government's fiscal, monetary, or regulatory policies that has lots of money running through it.

6. ACH (Accidental Cone Hollow). A cone with plant, equipment, and workers but little money, produced accidentally by the government's fiscal, monetary, or regulatory policies.

Short Answer/Fill-in/True or False

7. Accidental Cones are the cause of **recessions** and **depressions.**

8. The realization that Hollow Cones exist is especially important to **outside** sales people.

9. To qualify one's prospects means to discover whether there is a real, observable flow of money developing, or whether the money flow is simply a forecast (which may not materialize).

10. When you ask a businessperson the question "How's business?" you want to hear "Great! Sales this month are up X% over last month," *not* "Great! Production/Capital is up X% over last month." Increased sales are proof that a company is doing well, and most likely indicates a Filled/Filling Cone. An increase in production/capital may only signify that a company *plans* to do well, but this forecast may become a Hollow Cone.

11. True. A lot of investment is done on the basis of wishful thinking; so before you get involved in a cone, look for evidence of real flows of money.

Discussion/Essay/Assignment

12. Answers will vary.

Chapter 22: The Benefits of This Understanding

Define

1. Equity. The portion of a property held free and clear by the owner.

Short Answer/Fill-in/True or False

2. Uncle Eric advises Chris to warn friends and family about cones, especially Hollow Cones.

3. False: The Employment Act of 1946, the FDIC, Federal Reserve, and other government agencies are supposed to insure that a depression cannot happen, but they do not.

4. True. Small, localized depressions are common.

5. To best deal with small, localized depressions make the Clipper Ship Strategy a part of your life plan; always be ready to follow the dancing cones.

Chapter 23: Tax and Regulatory Cones

Define

1. Legislation. Made up law (political law), as distinct from scientific law, which is discovered law.

Short Answer/Fill-in/True or False:

2. Geographic areas in which firms receive various tax breaks and regulatory exemptions are called **enterprise zones**.

3. True. Changes in taxes and regulations confuse the market's natural steering mechanism of supply, demand, and price.

4. Changes in taxes reshape the cone/sinkhole landscape by turning the landscape into mountains and chasms, rather than by maintaining gently rolling hills and plains.

Chapter 24: Marginality

Define

1. Marginality. The "straw that broke the camel's back"—tiny changes in taxes or regulations thousands of miles away can have severe, unforeseeable consequences on you or the people to whom you sell your goods or services

2. Runaway Inflation. A hyperinflation. Prices rising rapidly, every few days or hours.

Short Answer/Fill-in/True or False

3. A tiny change in a tax or regulation can have an enormous effect on you due to the economic principle of marginality.

4. True. Any new tax or other change in political law, no matter how small, will create a sinkhole.

5. **Inflation** is probably the most effective method of building a cone by creating thousands of little-noticed sinkholes.

Discussion/Essay

6. Answers will vary, but should include the three points discussed in this chapter on Marginality.

Chapter 25: Marketing Managers

Define

1. Anomalies. A strange exception to what would be expected.

Short Answer/Fill-in/True or False

2. False. Businesses do not need to stay in one location and sell to people in that same location. Many types of businesses can stay in one location and sell all over the country. Examples include mail order companies, magazine/newsletter publishers, Internet companies, and computer software firms.

3. Uncle Eric advises Chris to enter into businesses that can stay in one location but sell all over the country without having to physically relocate because this type of business can always reach filled cones, moving its areas of focus to new filled cones when old ones become hollow.

Chapter 26: The Automobile

Define

1. Commodities. Raw materials. Natural resources. Basic materials traded on commodity markets. Examples: copper, lumber, soybeans, oil, gold, silver, aluminum, wheat, corn.

Short Answer/Fill-in/True or False

2. The automobile helps lessen the severity of chaos and hardships produced by dancing cones because people can use their automobiles to commute long distances, thus enabling them to better follow the dancing cones.

Chapter 27: How to Follow the Cones

Short Answer/Fill-in/True or False

1. The successful firms of yesterday were those who sought customers with incomes that were **large.** The successful firms of tomorrow will be those that seek customers with incomes that are **reliable.**

Discussion/Essay/Assignment

2. Answers will vary.

Chapter 28: A Case Study: Sacramento

Discussion/Essay/Assignment

1. Answers will vary.

Chapter 29: Hot Spots and Zips

Short Answer/Fill-in/True or False

1. True. No matter how bad general business conditions become in the country as a whole, there are always cones somewhere.

2. The digits in a zip code are organized to focus on geographic targets around the country. The first digit indicates one of ten large national areas encompassing several states; the second indicates a state, a portion of a heavily populated state, or two or more less populated states; the third stands for a major mailing center; the fourth and fifth indicate a local mailing station.

Discussion/Essay/Assignment

3. Answers will vary.

Chapter 30: The Importance of a Model for Sorting Your Data

Define

1. Gross National Product (GNP). The sum of all final goods and services produced in a nation. Does not include intermediate goods. Example: A car is a final good; the steel it contains is an intermediate good.

2. Accidental Cone Hollow (ACH). A cone with plant, equipment, and workers but little money.

3. Accidental Cone Filled (ACF). A cone that has lots of money running through it.

Short Answer/Fill-in/True or False

4. False. The correct statement is: Economic chaos leads to a desperate search for ways to cope, which leads to a desperate search for information.

5. To know which data are important and which are not, keep in mind a picture or model of how the world works; then, when you receive a new bit of information you can determine where the information fits with the model—or if it fits the model at all.

6. The big challenge is not so much in finding data to use, but in **deciding which data not to use.**

7. BCM/The Clipper Ship Strategy provides a **model** for selecting and processing the correct data.

Discussion/Essay

8. Answers will vary.

Chapter 31: Cone Classification

Discussion/Essay

1. Example: Grocery Store XYZ in Smalltown, CA

   a. Find out exactly who the customers are. *Anyone living in Smalltown, CA.*

   b. Find out exactly what they want. *Quality groceries and service at an affordable price.*

   c. Find a way to acquire or produce it. *Contact grocery distributors, start receiving inventory. Hire hard-working and courteous employees.*

   d. Tell them you can supply it to them. *Advertise in the Smalltown Newspaper; set up a billboard by the side of the road.*

   e. Remind them of the benefits to them. *Constantly illustrate to the customers, in advertisements and through the service and products provided, that Grocery Store XYZ provides quality groceries and service at an affordable price.*

   f. Ask for the money. *Checkout registers allow customers to pay for the groceries they buy.*

   Grocery Store XYZ falls into the "Non-Durables" industry and thus is insensitive to boom and bust cycles (aka, it has low cyclicality).

Chapter 32: Is Pinpoint Accuracy Necessary?

Short Answer/Fill-in/True or False

1. If a firm is the type that sells high value goods or services to a small number of people, you would want to classify your customers with great individual accuracy because it is important to know as much about your customers as possible since you only have a small number of them and they may be repeat customers.

2. If your firm is the type that sells inexpensive items to a large number of occasional one-type customers, you would want to classify your customers broadly because it would not be cost-effective or necessary to find out details about your customers since they are one-time buyers of low-cost items. Simply knowing a generalization about your customer base as a whole would be adequate.

3. True. If you are someone's employee, you personally are a firm with one customer. Your employer is your customer.

Chapter 33: How to Classify Cones

Define

1. DCF1. A Deliberate Cone, Federally created and first (1st) in line at the federal spigot (which is backed by the federal printing press.) These are people who have extremely steady, reliable incomes. Examples are retirees receiving Social Security, military pensioners, and civil service pensioners. These people vote and they have a great deal of political clout. Chances of their cones going dry are virtually nil. If you had a business and your firm's customers were all DCF1s, you could safely plan five or ten years into the future. Luck would play a very small part in your sales, and your success would be almost totally dependent on your skills. DCF1s are the highest quality cones, and if there is any way for you to build them into your customer base, you should expend great efforts to do so. Their stability will make life much easier for you.

2. DCF2. A Deliberate Cone, Federally created and second (2nd) in line at the federal spigot. Examples are federal agencies or employees. These are very good cones because their incomes are straight from the federal spigot and backed by the printing press. However, these people occasionally experience the budget cuts, layoffs, and career changes that have little effect on DC1s, so they are not as stable or reliable as DC1s.

3. DCF3. A Deliberate Cone, Federally created and third (3rd) in line at the federal spigot. This is a firm or individual who earns his living selling directly to DCF1s and DCF2s. Examples would be military contractors, retailers located just outside the gates of military

bases, and group insurance companies selling policies to federal employees. DCF3s can be valuable customers because their incomes do not fluctuate with the business cycle, but do not grow too dependent on them. They can be affected by federal budget cuts and layoffs.

4. ACF. An Accidental Cone Filled. A cone that has lots of money running through it.

5. ACH. An Accidental Cone Hollow. A cone with plant, equipment, and workers but little money.

6. S (Sinkhole). A depressed area. An area from which more wealth is removed than is poured back in.

Short Answer/Fill-in/True or False

7. For each person or firm you are trying to classify, ask these two questions:
   a. Is this person or firm a Deliberate Cone (DC) or an Accidental Cone (AC)?
   b. Are they Filled (F) or Hollow (H)?

8. The Deliberate Cone (DC) is the better customer because he has a more reliable income than the Accidental Cone Filled (ACF). The ACF may have more money for the moment but cannot be counted on in the long run.

9. True. Your DCs are your source of stability and your ACFs are your source of large profits.

10. **DCs** are resistant to changes in the Federal Reserve's monetary policy and **ACs** are not.

11. False. The correct statement is: You should target ACFs because when the money supply is expanding rapidly (or money demand is falling) ACFs grow rapidly. Be aggressive and take advantage of these ACFs, *but don't rely on them in the long run because an ACFs lifespan may be short, always have a stable back-up.*

12. Uncle Eric believes most people can get by using the following four categories for classification: DC, ACF, ACH, and S.

Discussion/Essay

13. Answers will vary.

Chapter 34: Precision and Size of Firm

Short Answer/Fill-in/True or False

1. Generally, a small firm requires greater precision than a large firm.

2. If you do not know whether a cone is a DC or an AC, assume it is **AC**; if you do not know whether it is Filled or Hollow, assume it is **Hollow**. You should err on the side of caution because it will keep you from becoming dependent on cones that are less stable than they appear. You will avoid a false sense of security and be better able to prepare for a sudden drop in your income.

Chapter 35: Split Cones

Define

1. Split Cones (SC). Cones that fall between Deliberate and Accidental Cones.

2. Accidental Cone Exporter (ACE). A cone produced accidentally by the government's fiscal, monetary, or regulatory policies that derives its income from sales abroad.

3. Accidental Cone Importer (ACI). A cone produced accidentally by the government's fiscal, monetary, or regulatory policies, which derives its income from sales of goods purchased abroad.

4. Business cycle Insensitive (I). Income only slightly affected by the boom-and-bust cycle.

5. Somewhat business cycle sensitive (Sw). Income affected by the boom-and-bust cycle, but not seriously.

6. Very business cycle sensitive (V). Income seriously affected by the boom-and-bust cycle.

Short Answer/Fill-in/True or False

7. Sensitivity to the business cycle can be determined based on the purchasing behavior of the cone's customers.

8. Examples of businesses that are *sensitive* to the business cycle include: auto manufacturers, swimming pool contractors and subcontractors, housing construction, real estate companies.

    Examples of businesses that are *insensitive* to business cycles include: a government spending program, food suppliers of staple food products, water companies, electric companies, gasoline companies, trash collection companies, phone companies.

Chapter 36: An Eerie Feeling

Assignment

1. Answers will vary.

Chapter 37: Gathering More Information

Short Answer/Fill-in/True or False

1. Answers will vary, but the primary reason for having prize drawings using business cards is that the information on the business cards will tell the business owner the *occupations* of the customers, thus providing information to help in classification.

Chapter 38: Specialized Organizations and Publications

Assignment

1. Answers will vary.

Chapter 39: External Information—A D.E.W. Line

Define

1. Distant Early Warning Line (D.E.W. Line). A system of information sources capable of tracking the health and location of your cones. This way, anything that affects your cones will be detected before it can harm you. The term is taken from a line of radar stations constructed across Canada in the 1950s to watch for incoming Russian bombers.

2. Lobbyist. Origin of the term is from a person who hangs around the legislature lobby trying to secure the votes of lawmakers.

Short Answer/Fill-in/True or False

3. If you cannot find a newsletter or organization associated with a DC it generally means that the DC is not very healthy.

4. **Political law** is the greatest influence on any cone.

5. Answers will vary; for guidance, see Maybury's explanation found in this chapter.

Assignment

6. Answers will vary.

Chapter 40: S.I.C. Codes

Define

1. S.I.C. codes (Standard Industrial Classification codes). For data processing purposes, the federal government classifies each industry and occupation according to S.I.C. codes (Standard Industrial Classification codes).

2. House Organ. An internal company publication such as a newsletter for employees.

Assignment

3. Answers will vary.

Chapter 41: List Companies and Marketing Data

Short Answer/Fill-in/True or False

1. Answers will vary. In general, the DIRECT MAIL LIST CATALOG contains a list of companies selling names and addresses of potential customers. After locating a good cone, a businessperson can use the DIRECT MAIL LIST CATALOG to reach customers in that cone.

Chapter 42: Importance of Real Estate

Short Answer/Fill-in/True or False

1. True. Real estate is the best indicator of the location of cones and sinkholes. Real estate is generally the largest purchase anyone makes so it brings the greatest changes.

2. "Where property values are skyrocketing you will find a **cone**, and where they are falling you will find a **sinkhole**."

Chapter 43: Learn by Example

Short Answer/Fill-in/True or False

1. Answers will vary. See content of Chapter 43 for guidance.

Chapter 44: Sales Side Summary

Short Answer/Fill-in/True or False

1. The five main points (summary) of the sales strategy are:
   a. Identify the sources of your income.
   b. Classify these sources. Are they AC or DC? Filled or Hollow?
   c. Determine how vulnerable you are. What is your mix? % of ACF, % of ACH, % of DC, % of S.
   d. If you have a high concentration of ACs, try to get more DCs.
   e. During economic downturns, concentrate on DCs. During booms reach out to ACs but be ready to pull back at any time. ACs are extremely vulnerable to recessions.

Part 2: Production Strategy

Chapter 45: Stomping the Town

Short Answer/Fill-in/True or False

1. Answers will vary. Example: In movies, fictional monster Godzilla wrecks towns without rhyme or reason. So, too, can political law wreck towns without rhyme or reason. The best way to cope is by owning only those types of plant and equipment that can be hurriedly moved out of "Godzilla's" path.

Chapter 46: Your Factors of Production

Define

1. Factors of Production. Land, labor, capital, and entrepreneurship.

2. Land. In economics, includes not only terra firma but also the buildings, crops that might be growing on the land, minerals in it, or the fences around it. "Land" can also include rights to use sea lanes, or extract minerals from the sea or from under the sea, like oil.

3. Labor. Work. Also workers, in reference to unions.

4. Capital. The buildings, office equipment, and other tools workers need to produce what we want to buy, or, the money saved to buy these things.

5. Entrepreneur. The spark plug that makes the economy run. The person who searches for opportunities, takes risks, makes the important decisions and organizes land, labor, and capital. The essence of the firm.

Short Answer/Fill-in/True or False

6. Of the four factors of production (Land, Labor, Capital, Entrepreneurship), Uncle Eric believes entrepreneurship is most important because the entrepreneur is the spark plug that makes the economy run.

Chapter 47: Streamlining

Define

1. Streamlined. To shape for fast and easy movement.

Short Answer/Fill-in/True or False

2. To minimize risks and maximize profits in an environment of political law, you must be highly adaptable, which means you must be able to move instantly and quickly whenever conditions change. In other words, you must be *streamlined.* You must own as little land, labor, and capital as possible.

3. Ideally, in a government-controlled economy a firm should consist only of **the entrepreneur and his/her cash.**

4. Ideally, the only two roles the entrepreneur should perform are: organizer and coordinator.

5. True. In a land controlled by political law, the three keys to success are: mobility, mobility, and mobility.

Chapter 48: Cyclical Problems

Short Answer/Fill-in/True or False

1. When the economy is expanding, production is the major problem. Uncle Eric says, "You must expand fast enough to satisfy all the new demand, otherwise competitors will come in and crowd you out. This situation develops because the government can create money faster than you can create goods or services to soak up the money."

2. When the economy experiences a bust, marketing becomes the problem because, says Uncle Eric, "less money is being created, or the demand has increased, which means less is being spent, so entrepreneurs run into problems of excess production capacity."

3. False. Bankruptcies are *not* made during busts, they are made during booms; they only come to light in the busts.

Chapter 49: Break-Even Analysis

Define

1. Break-Even Analysis. Mathematical calculation showing the point at which a company's costs and income are exactly equal, the break-even point.

2. Fixed Costs. "Overhead"—utilities, taxes, insurance, and other costs that cannot be easily reduced.

3. Variable Costs. Those costs that increase incrementally as units are produced. These can include raw materials, electricity, production wages, transportation, and others. These are added to the fixed costs to determine the firm's total costs.

4. Rent. Fee paid for the temporary use of something.

5. Break-Even Point. When sales reach the point where all costs are covered and the firm begins earning profits with each unit sold thereafter.

Short Answer/Fill-in/True or False

6. Answers will vary but should follow the definitions outlined in this chapter.

Chapter 50: Mrs. Garcia

Define

1. Fascism. The belief that power holders should do whatever appears necessary, no exceptions, no limits. The political philosophy of the Roman Empire after about 31 BC.

Short Answer/Fill-in/True or False

2. Most Panamanians would either send their money out of Panama or hold it in a highly portable, concealable form, such as gold, diamonds, or dollars. Owners of plant/equipment protected these holdings by developing connections and influence in the government.

3. "Mrs. Garcia" taught Uncle Eric that Godzilla's behavior is not predictable—always be ready and able to get out of town fast.

Chapter 51: A New Industry

Define

1. De-industrialization. The process of allowing the risks of owning plant and equipment to be shifted onto others. Instead of being called de-industrialization, it is often called restructuring, or sale-leaseback, outsourcing, vertical disaggregation, dynamic networking, or something else.

Short Answer/Fill-in/True or False

2. "A good rule of thumb: If it cannot be easily sold at a good price during the next recession, **don't own it—rent it."**

3. "A better rule: Determine exactly what service it performs for you, then **purchase this service from someone else."**

4. Employee-leasing is one of America's fastest growing industries. Employee-leasing firms hire groups of workers for other firms to rent.

5. True. De-industrialization is caused by the existence of political law.

Assignment

6. Answers will vary.

Chapter 52: Break-Even Solutions

Define

1. Break-Even Flexibility. Making one's break-even point flexible so that if income slides downward, the break-even point can be slid downward, too.

2. Payback Analysis. The procedure for determining the time required to recover the cost of a specific investment — the payback.

Short Answer/Fill-in/True or False

3. Three ways to solve break-even problems as outlined by Uncle Eric are:

    a. Acquire DC sources of income.

    b. Make the break-even point flexible so that if income slides downward the break-even point can be slid downward, too.

    c. Make the break-even point flexible and acquire DC sources of income to cover whatever is inflexible.

4. If a recession or some other political catastrophe cuts your income, you can more quickly move to a smaller, less expensive structure if you rent rather than own or lease.

5. When a recession hits and sales drop off, you can reduce your debt burden along with sales if you have restricted the use of debt financing to variable costs—for example, inventory.

6. Many firms get into financial trouble when they launch a long-term project when monetary policy is loose, but this can turn catastrophic when monetary policy becomes tight.

Chapter 53: The Most Risky Investment

Short Answer/Fill-in/True or False

1. According to Uncle Eric, the most risky investment is real estate because it is the most illiquid investment.

Chapter 54: Specialization

Define

1. Specialization of Labor. Each individual spending most of his work time on a single job.

2. Scientific Law. Verbal or mathematical expressions of Natural Law learned through observation, study, and experimentation.

Short Answer/Fill-in/True or False

3. In an environment of political law, the big dollars are earned by the **traders,** not the **producers**.

Chapter 55: Payback Analysis

Short Answer/Fill-in/True or False

1. Payback is the time required to recover the cost of a specific investment.

2. False. The correct statement is: The higher the payback percentage, the less risk because you get your money back faster.

3. In a business, generally earlier investments have better paybacks than later investments.

Chapter 56: Start-Up Firms: An Example

Short Answer/Fill-in/True or False

1. The Horatio Alger model would start with production, the BCM model would start with research and sales by finding a healthy cone.

Chapter 57: Careers in BCM

Short Answer/Fill-in/True or False

1. As long as political law is present in their personal and business lives, it is in the best interest of business owners to identify stable cones. Being able to reliably classify his/her customer base helps the businessperson realize how stable and reliable the customers' incomes will be and, consequently, project sales. Providing a BCM consulting service helps the businessperson acquire this important customer information.

Chapter 58: Investment Strategy

Short Answer/Fill-in/True or False

1. Uncle Eric says the best long-term investment plan is to have no long-term investment plan.

2. The purpose of savings is capital preservation.

3. According to Uncle Eric, you should commit funds for speculation only when you've located a cone.

4. True. Uncle Eric says to always be diversified, never put all your eggs in one basket.

Chapter 59: Two Types of Investment Cones

Define

1. Double Cone Investment. One that earns profits through two flows of money—capital gains and earnings. Examples of doubles are stocks, bonds, and commercial real estate. All earn money through their daily operations, and we also hope they rise in value, earning more money through capital gains.

2. Capital Gain. A capital gain is an increase in the value of the investment, as when a stock rises.

3. Single Cone Investments. Those that earn profits only through capital gains. Examples are commodities, undeveloped land, currencies, art, and antiques.

Short Answer/Fill-in/True or False

4. Rothschild avoided losses by being cautious. He knew that getting out a year too early was better than getting out a day too late.

Chapter 60: Summary

Final Assignment

1. Letters will vary, but the student should cover the eight summary points from this chapter.

Final Exam Answers

1. The business cycle is the "boom-and-bust" cycle of inflationary expansions and deflationary contractions or recessions.

2. Business Cycle Management (BCM) is an investment strategy that shows business managers and sales people how to take advantage of the fact that pockets of prosperity can be discovered and tapped into, no matter how good or bad business conditions may be.

3. Wealth is goods and services — food, clothing, haircuts, cars, TVs, homes, and everything else that makes life better. Not to be confused with money. Money can be wealth, but it is only one kind. Money is the tool we use to measure and trade wealth. As long as a person has wealth, money is a minor consideration.

4. A model is a mental picture of how the world works. Models are how we think; models are how we understand how the world works. Models help us sort and prioritize information — they help us know what information is important and what information is not.

5. The discount rate is an interest rate and one of the Federal Reserve's tools for manipulating the money supply. A rising rate means a restricted money supply, and a falling rate means a rising money supply.

6. To get the "real" money supply, subtract price increases from money supply increases.

7. A forecast is a *prediction based on analysis of available data.* Evidence is *facts that tend to verify.*

8. Austrian economics is the most free market economic viewpoint today.

9. Most economists from schools other than Austrian economics assume that the economy is a giant machine. Austrian economists see the economy not as a machine but as an *ecology* since it is made up of organisms—people.

10. Line Functions are sales and production. Staff Functions provide support for the Line Functions (accounting, finance, legal, personnel, administration, etc.). The Production Functions are the parts of a firm that create the goods or services. Sales Function is the activity of trading a firm's goods or services for money.

11. The Clipper Ship Strategy is a system to locate where there is a pile of money, tap into that pile (knowing the pile will not last forever), while continuing to search for new piles.

12. Sales and production are the two primary functions every business performs.

13. The four important rules for achieving success as demonstrated by the story of the extreme clipper are: 1) Find out where there is a pile of money; 2) Tap into that pile; 3) Don't expect the pile to last forever; 4) Always be searching for new piles.

14. People who are not early recipients of the money that is injected into the economy are hurt by the situation because their incomes do not rise as quickly as prices rise.

15. False. In the early stages of inflation, it usually takes the money a long time, sometimes years, to spread to its maximum limits.

16. False. Political law can change at any time without warning, which means that the flow of money can also change without warning.

17. True. The economy cannot be stable unless law is stable.

18. False. Most of the money in "cones" is old money that has been in the economy for a long time. Then the government scoops it out, in the form of tax collections, and mixes it with newly created money.

19. In the United States today, political law determines the location of cones.

20. Washington D.C. is the most stable cone in the world.

21. Named after swindler Charles Ponzi, a Ponzi scheme is one in which investors are paid not from income earned by the investment but from the contributions of new investors. Ponzis go broke when the number of new investors is no longer great enough to support the earlier investors. This is also called a pyramid scheme.

22. The U.S. government's social security program is the biggest, most stable cone.

23. The idea of Social Security as an insurance program was "sold" to Congress and the American public in 1935.

24. Some of the problems created by Social Security include: Social Security does not *produce* income, it only *transfers* income; Social Security does not create factories or office buildings or jobs for the young; Social Security actually *erases* jobs for the young, and contributes to the difficulty young people have in getting ahead; When someone today spends Social Security money, he/she is consuming not only his/her children's tax money, but their jobs, too.

25. A Deliberate Cone is a cone created directly by government agencies injecting money into the economy in specific, *planned* locations.

26. An Accidental Cone is a cone produced accidentally by the government's fiscal, monetary, or regulatory policies.

27. A Natural Cones is an area in which the supply of money is increasing due to normal increases in demand for a good or service, not due to injections of money by the government.

28. True: Accidental Cones can be extremely profitable but also extremely dangerous if you do not know how to handle them.

29. In a free economy, the cone/sinkhole landscape tends *not* to be very rugged because the invisible hand works to smooth them out before they get very large.

30. An entrepreneur is the spark plug that makes the economy run—the person who searches for opportunities, takes risks, makes the important decisions, and *organizes* land, labor, and capital—the essence of the firm.

31. Accidental Cones are more common and typically larger and more profitable than Deliberate Cones.

32. When a firm's sales start dropping it is a sign the flow of money might be slowing, so be cautious because a cone may be about to turn into a sinkhole.

33. A sales boom is a safer, less-risky investment because it is caused by a real flow of money.

34. Capital: the buildings, office equipment, and other tools workers need to produce what we want to buy; or, the money saved to buy these things.

35. Accidental Cones are the cause of **recessions** and **depressions**.

36. True. Changes in taxes and regulations confuse the market's natural steering mechanism of supply, demand, and price.

37. True. Inflation is probably the most effective method of building a cone by creating thousands of little-noticed sinkholes.

38. True. No matter how bad general business conditions become in the country as a whole, there are always cones somewhere.

39. Gross National Product (GNP). The sum of all final goods and services produced in a nation. Does not include intermediate goods. Example: A car is a final good; the steel it contains is an intermediate good.

40. To know which data are important and which are not, keep in mind a picture or *model* of how the world works; then, when you receive a new bit of information you can determine where the information fits with the model—or if it fits the model.

41. True. If you are someone's employee, you personally are a firm with one customer. Your employer is your customer.

42. The Deliberate Cone (DC) is the better customer because he has a more reliable income than the Accidental Cone Filled (ACF). The ACF may have more money for the moment but cannot be counted on in the long run.

43. **Political law** is the greatest influence on any cone.

44. True. Real estate is the best indicator of the location of cones and sinkholes.

45. According to Uncle Eric, "Where property values are skyrocketing you will find a **cone,** and where they are falling you will find a **sinkhole**."

46. The four factors of production are **land, labor, capital,** and **entrepreneurship.**

47. Of the four factors of production (Land, Labor, Capital, Entrepreneurship), Uncle Eric believes entrepreneurship is most important because the entrepreneur is the spark plug that makes the economy run.

48. To minimize risks and maximize profits in an environment of political law, you must be highly adaptable, which means you must be able to move instantly and quickly whenever conditions change. In other words, you must be *streamlined*—own as little land, labor, and capital as possible.

49. True. In a land controlled by political law, the three keys to success are: mobility, mobility, and mobility.

50. Break-Even Point. When sales reach the point where all costs are covered and the firm begins earning profits with each unit sold thereafter.

51. De-industrialization. The process of allowing the risks of owning plant and equipment to be shifted onto others. Instead of being called de-industrialization, it is often called restructuring, or sale-leaseback, outsourcing, vertical disaggregation, dynamic networking, or something else.

52. According to Uncle Eric, the most risky investment is real estate because it is the most illiquid investment.

53. In an environment of political law, the big dollars are earned by the **traders**, not the **producers**.

54. False. The correct statement is: The higher the payback percentage, the *less* risk because you get your money back faster.

55. According to Uncle Eric, you should commit funds for speculation only when you've located a cone.

Thought Exercises Revisited (This can be an oral or written exercise.)

56. Before the student began to read THE CLIPPER SHIP STRATEGY the student was asked to answer the Thought Exercises on page 11 of this Study Guide. Now that the student has finished reading THE CLIPPER SHIP STRATEGY, the student has been asked to review the answers to the Thought Exercises and change any answers based on new knowledge learned as a result of reading THE CLIPPER SHIP STRATEGY.

Has the student made any changes to his/her original responses? If so, make sure the student used logic and accurately applied concepts and ideas from the text, THE CLIPPER SHIP STRATEGY.

If the student made no change, did the student explain why he/she was satisfied with the original answer as previously written?

If the student did not originally provide an answer for lack of knowledge, is the answer now provided by the student consistent with the concepts learned in THE CLIPPER SHIP STRATEGY?

Published by Bluestocking Press

Uncle Eric Books by Richard J. Maybury

UNCLE ERIC TALKS ABOUT PERSONAL, CAREER, AND FINANCIAL SECURITY
WHATEVER HAPPENED TO PENNY CANDY?
WHATEVER HAPPENED TO JUSTICE?
ARE YOU LIBERAL? CONSERVATIVE? OR CONFUSED?
ANCIENT ROME: HOW IT AFFECTS YOU TODAY
EVALUATING BOOKS: WHAT WOULD THOMAS JEFFERSON THINK ABOUT THIS?
THE MONEY MYSTERY
THE CLIPPER SHIP STRATEGY
THE THOUSAND YEAR WAR IN THE MIDEAST
WORLD WAR I: THE REST OF THE STORY
WORLD WAR II: THE REST OF THE STORY

Bluestocking Guides (study guides for the Uncle Eric books)
by Jane A. Williams and/or Kathryn Daniels

A BLUESTOCKING GUIDE: BUILDING A PERSONAL MODEL FOR SUCCESS (based on UNCLE ERIC TALKS ABOUT...)
A BLUESTOCKING GUIDE: ECONOMICS (based on WHATEVER HAPPENED TO PENNY CANDY?)
A BLUESTOCKING GUIDE: JUSTICE (based on WHATEVER HAPPENED TO JUSTICE?)
A BLUESTOCKING GUIDE: POLITICAL PHILOSOPHIES (based on ARE YOU LIBERAL? CONSERVATIVE? OR CONFUSED?)
A BLUESTOCKING GUIDE: ANCIENT ROME (based on ANCIENT ROME: HOW IT AFFECTS YOU TODAY)
A BLUESTOCKING GUIDE: SOLVING THE MONEY MYSTERY (based on THE MONEY MYSTERY)
A BLUESTOCKING GUIDE: APPLYING THE CLIPPER SHIP STRATEGY (based on THE CLIPPER SHIP STRATEGY)
A BLUESTOCKING GUIDE: THE MIDEAST WAR (based on THE THOUSAND YEAR WAR IN THE MIDEAST)
A BLUESTOCKING GUIDE: WORLD WAR I: THE REST OF THE STORY
A BLUESTOCKING GUIDE: WORLD WAR II: THE REST OF THE STORY

Each Study Guide includes some or all of the following:
    1) chapter-by-chapter comprehension questions and answers
    2) application questions and answers
    3) research activities
    4) essay assignments
    5) thought questions
    6) final exam

More Bluestocking Press Titles

LAURA INGALLS WILDER AND ROSE WILDER LANE HISTORICAL TIMETABLE
ECONOMICS: A FREE MARKET READER edited by Jane Williams & Kathryn Daniels
CAPITALISM FOR KIDS: GROWING UP TO BE YOUR OWN BOSS by Karl Hess
BUSINESS FOR KIDS: EXPLAINING COMMON SENSE REALITIES BEHIND BASIC BUSINESS PRINCIPLES
    by Kathryn Daniels & Anthony Joseph

The Bluestocking Press Catalog
Includes varied and interesting selections of historical toys and crafts, historical documents, economics, and more.

Order any of the above items from Bluestocking Press by phone or online.

Bluestocking Press
web site: www.BluestockingPress.com
Phone: 800-959-8586
email: CustomerService@BluestockingPress.com